alex m

MW01032594

10 Questions
every christian must answer

thoughtful responses to
strengthen your faith

ACADEMIC

NASHVILLE, TENNESSEE

ISBN: 978-1-4336-7181-4

Published by B&H Publishing Group
Nashville, Tennessee

Dewey Decimal Classification: 234.2
Subject Heading: FAITH \ CHRISTIAN LIFE \ DOCTRINAL
THEOLOGY

4 5 6 7 8 9 • 15 14 13 12 11
R

IN APPRECIATION

In appreciation to Mrs. Linda Elliott, my editorial assistant, who re-typed my chapters, edited them more than once, and proofread and formatted the footnotes.

To my constant research assistant who always gives me more data than I need, who is available 365/24, who is patient to pursue data when I lose my notes, and my counselor and teacher—thanks to Google.

After spending thirty years answering questions sent to Jerry Falwell, I realize Christians have questions; God has answers and He uses the Bible to enlighten any who seek answers to the hard questions in life.

Elmer L. Towns, cofounder
and dean, School of Religion
Liberty University

The following people have greatly assisted me in the writing of my portions of this book: Stephanie Roberts, a very gifted graduate student at Southern Evangelical Seminary; Christina Woodside, writing instructor, resourceful assistant, and proofreader par excellence; Richard Howe, Ph.D., who provided some key research on the chapter dealing with the origin of the universe.

Very special thanks are due to Mr. Tom Neven, who helped format and clarify this work.

I am deeply grateful for Dr. Elmer Towns, who has been to me a Sunday school teacher, professor, friend, and now collaborator. He has excelled in all of these roles.

Most of all, I am thankful to the Lord Jesus Christ, who has allowed me to experience the joy of salvation and the privilege of service.

Alex McFarland, former president
Southern Evangelical Seminary, speaker, and broadcaster

Contents

Preface

We have written *Ten Questions Every Christian Must Answer* because each question involves an attack on Christianity. These questions begin with the age-old inquiry about the existence of truth and end with the knotty question about hell.

Is There Such a Thing as Absolute Truth? (Alex McFarland)

How Can I Know There Is a God? (Alex McFarland)

Where Did the Universe Come From? (Alex McFarland)

Is the Bible Reliable? (Elmer Towns)

Is Jesus the Only Way? (Elmer Towns)

Are the Claims of Jesus' Physical Resurrection from the Dead Valid? (Alex McFarland)

Are the Heathen Really Lost? (Elmer Towns)

Is Hell a Real Place That Lasts for Eternity? (Alex McFarland)

Must a Person Believe in Jesus or Make Him Lord of His life to Be Saved? (Elmer Towns)

How Detailed Is God's Wonderful Plan for Each Individual Life? (Elmer Towns)

Conclusion: Truth in Real Life (Alex McFarland)

The answers to these ten questions will give you ammunition to use with the unsaved. However, you may need these answers more than they. Many Christians need answers to confirm their faith that Christianity is right. Also these answers may be needed to share when someone challenges your faith. These answers will help you deal kindly with someone (Christian or non-Christian) who is confused about Christianity.

But some people do not want answers. They are not seeking truth. They have their minds made up and perhaps they throw questions at you to destroy your faith.

Some skeptics like to argue for the sake of arguing. You answer one question, and they have another question. Some have their agenda settled and they "don't want to be confused by the facts." Maybe some skeptics are God-rejecters; they argue because they have rejected God with their hearts (their emotions and belief system). They don't want answers; they want to win an argument.

Skeptics probably do not need answers; they need a relationship with a believer who will reach them where they are and lift them to God. They may need to see "Christ in you, the hope of glory" (Col 1:27). When they are convinced that you live with integrity, then they will listen.

What is our *authority*? Some unsaved friends won't listen to rational explanations. They first need a loving relationship before a believer can present an answer to the questions in this book.

But some questions do not come from the frustration of academic problems. Some people may have an honest straightforward question (e.g., "What must I do to be saved?" [Acts 16:30]). They may have a probing question (e.g., "How can anyone be born when he is old? . . . Can he enter his mother's womb a second time and be born?" [John 3:4]). These seekers need answers from Scripture, with an explanation.

The attitude that you the reader bring to the questions in this book is important. If we demonstrated intellectually there is a God, would you accept His existence? Would you turn to Him for salvation? If you were convinced He is the Creator, and you were a creation of His hands, would you obey His commands?

Perhaps you come to these questions knowing there is a God, and that you are His child. But some of these questions perplex you; or some questions may even irritate you. Then you are a seeker—maybe a wounded seeker who needs logical answers to these questions.

Each chapter includes a section called *POINT.* This is a statement of what Christians have always believed and how they look at the question.

Each chapter also includes *COUNTERPOINT,* the beliefs of those who reject the Christian answer. The *COUNTERPOINT* is the reason some attack Christianity with this protracted question. Following *COUNTERPOINT* are the reasons why skeptics reject Christian answers, and/or the arguments by the skeptic for their point of view. If we do not recognize and answer the arguments of skeptics, then we cannot help them nor can we strengthen our faith.

Getting a Grip on the Term *Apologetics*

The questions (and those asking them) deserve good answers. I (Alex) often make the following statement in my opening remarks to audiences: "The claims of Christianity are affirmed by compelling lines of evidence. The positive evidence for Christianity sets it apart from all other faith systems." College students especially are intrigued by such claims and by the content that follows.

But whether the questions relate to truth, God's existence and nature, the Bible, Jesus Christ, or the question of why God would allow pain and suffering in the world—Christianity does have a threefold advantage: (a) positive evidence points in its favor, (b) no legitimate negative evidence exists to refute it, and (c) the objections raised against Christianity can be satisfactorily answered.

The work of making a positive case for Christianity or making a negative case against its challenges is *apologetics*.

This discipline deals with a rational defense of Christianity. It gives a reason or justification of one's beliefs, and presents evidences and sound reasoning to reach individuals for Christ.

A Spiritual Discipline for Our Times

Christian thinker G. K. Chesterton observed in 1933 that while it is important to win the unsaved to Christianity, leaders must increasingly endeavor to "convert the *Christians* to Christianity." Chesterton's remark was a timeless reminder that the church must be ever dedicated in its duty to pass on biblical truth to rising generations.

Today more belief systems than ever are competing for the attention of people. Because of this, we believe it is vital for churches to incorporate apologetics and worldview content into their ministries. "Worldview" refers to *what* a person believes. "Apologetics" is all about *why* one believes the things he believes. Individuals within the church—and those on the outside possibly looking in—need to learn about both.

The Greek word for apologetics appears several times in the Bible. Usually translated as "answer" and "reason," *apologia* means "a defense." A few of the categories of Christian apologetics include the following: (1) *textual apologetics*—defending the trustworthiness of the Bible and then presenting the content of what it says; (2) *evidence-based apologetics*—presenting external data that provide objective confirmation of the Christian faith (such as historical or scientific facts); and (3) *philosophical apologetics*—exposing the flawed reasoning behind popular arguments against Christianity.

Much has been written about the decades-long erosion of Christianity in America and the West. The challenges to Christianity are even causing some church members to ponder how Christianity stacks up against competing beliefs. Statements like "You've got your truth and I've got mine," or "Jesus was just one of many great spiritual leaders" have become axiomatic in our culture. Knowledge of apologetics helps both Christians and non-Christians understand why the claims of Christianity are to be preferred rather than those of some other belief system.

Why not just embrace the atheism insisted on by books like Richard Dawkins's *The God Delusion?* The answer is multifaceted. But Christianity is to be believed and followed because it is *true*. In a world of sincerely held opinions, Christianity comes via historical, yet personally relevant, *facts*.

Protecting Those Who May Be Spiritually Vulnerable

A recent video showed some footage from Africa in which a baby water buffalo was rescued from the mouths of three hungry lions. The people whose camcorder captured this could be heard cheering as one adult water buffalo courageously fought off the lions. The video reminded me (Alex) that within the world are predators, prey, and protectors. Believers need to be equipped for the intellectual questions and spiritual challenges that inevitably come. Apologetics content helps by demonstrating that Christianity is credible, reasonable, and relevant.

Some pastors shy away from teaching apologetics, assuming that their people will not understand it or that it is a pursuit for just the super intelligent. To such sentiments, I respectfully object! For nearly 20 years I have witnessed people of all ages and economic strata react to apologetics content with enthusiasm and appreciation. One of the reactions that I (Alex) often hear is "Alex, all of this has helped me see that Christianity really *makes sense.*" Yes, it does. The best part is that once people get a handle on understanding, explaining, and defending the faith, they are more likely than ever to reach out to their friends. Apologetics encourages (and equips) the saved and is often used by the Holy Spirit to persuade the lost.

All New Testament Occurrences of the Term from Which Is Derived the Word "Apologetics"

The following eight verses from the New Testament all include the Greek word *apologeo,* a legal term that means "to speak in defense of."

Acts 22:1

"Brothers and fathers, listen now to my *defense.*"

Acts 25:16

"I answered them that it's not the Romans' custom to give any man up before the accused confronts the accusers face to face and has an opportunity to give a *defense* concerning the charge."

1 Corinthians 9:3

"My *defense* to those who examine me is this."

2 Corinthians 7:11

"For consider how much diligence this very thing—this grieving as God wills—has produced in you: what a *desire* to clear yourselves, what indignation, what fear, what deep longing, what zeal, what

justice! In every way you have commended yourselves to be pure
in this matter."

Philippians 1:7

"It is right for me to think this way about all of you, because I have
you in my heart, and you are all partners with me in grace, both
in my imprisonment and in the *defense* and establishment of the
gospel."

Philippians 1:16

These do so out of love, knowing that I am appointed for the
defense of the gospel. "

2 Timothy 4:16

"At my first *defense*, no one came to my assistance, but everyone
deserted me. May it not be counted against them."

1 Peter 3:15

"But set apart the Messiah as Lord in your hearts, and always be
ready to give a *defense* to anyone who asks you for a reason for the
hope that is in you."

Apologetics in the New Testament

In the verses listed above the word *defense* implies validation of
one's position and explanation and affirmation of something, especially when put under the light of scrutiny. In 1 Pet 3:15 (perhaps
the most famous verse associated with the discipline of apologetics), the word that jumps out is *defense*. Many translations render
the word *apologia* in this verse as "answer," which is also appropriate. The phrase "for a reason" comes from a different Greek root,
yet still carries the implication of a *reasoned, logical* approach. As

stated in the definition above, apologetics involves the use of evidences and sound reasoning to reach individuals for Christ.

A verse that does not include the word *apologia*—yet one which definitely deserves notice—is in the book of Jude. Of Jude's 25 brief verses, verse 3 admonishes believers to "contend for the faith." Some translations of Jude 3 may read "defend the faith," or "strive strongly for the faith," or something similar. The word translated "contend" in English comes from a word that can mean to struggle for something. The Greek word also is the basis for the word *agonize*. The implication is that with consistency, effectiveness, and absolute dedication, each Christian is to stand up for this precious message, "the faith once delivered to the saints."

In introducing apologetics to audiences who may be hearing about it for the first time, I often say, "There was only one apostle Paul, and he was an apologist." A careful reading of the book of Acts makes it hard to miss Paul's skill as an apologist/evangelist.

In Thessalonica Paul *"reasoned* with them from the Scriptures, *explaining* and *showing* that the Messiah had to suffer and rise from the dead, and saying, "This is the Messiah, Jesus, whom I am proclaiming to you" (Acts 17:2–3). In his quest to make a presentation of the gospel that was both understandable and persuasive, Paul was explaining and defending his content before the Greek listeners. The word in verse 3 translated "reasoned" is the word from which stems "dialogue."

The word *explaining* means "discussing" or even "disputing." And the word *demonstrating* can also mean "to open up" (something). When a Christian presents, explains, or defends the gospel, his hope is that people will become more favorably inclined to the message, and to become *open* to the reality of Jesus Christ!

This same word for "showing" is found in a few other New Testament passages. In Mark 7 we read of Jesus' healing a man who was both deaf and mute. In verse 34, Jesus prayed for the man, saying, "Be opened!" This same word in Acts 17:3 speaks of Paul "demonstrating." Jesus gave hearing and speech to a destitute man. To people who may be spiritually destitute, believers are to give a clear "demonstration" (an "opening"). The approach to apologetics should be like that of Paul—something that makes a "clear demonstration" or yields a decisive "opening up."

What Apologetics Is *Not*

More than a few times I have had someone say to me, "Alex, I don't *apologize* for being a Christian!" Moments before speaking at a major denominational seminary recently, one of the school's faculty was escorting me around and said, "I heard them say you are an apologist. What are you apologizing for?"

Since even some pastors and seminary staff are unfamiliar with the subject, let it be stated, *apologetics is not about saying "I'm sorry."* Actually the words "I'm sorry" are traceable to the Latin phrase "mea culpa." A "mea culpa" is an admission of guilt, as if to say, "I am culpable; I am guilty." And this has absolutely *nothing* to do with Christian apologetics.

No one needs assume that the apologist is somehow waving the white flag of surrender on behalf of Christianity. Apologetics does not mean to say "I'm sorry " for anything about our faith. Quite the opposite! The apologist is showing that we have an authentic *message*. But we must also make sure that we present ourselves as authentic *messengers*.

Shortly after I became president of Southern Evangelical Seminary in North Carolina, a pastor shared a story with me that nearly broke my heart. I was encouraging this pastor to bring more apologetics and biblical worldview content before his people, and I could tell he was "guarded."

xvi 10 QUESTIONS EVERY CHRISTIAN MUST ANSWER

The pastor explained that a two-man apologetics team had come one Sunday night to speak to their youth. During a question-and-answer time, a teen girl innocently asked a question about Jehovah's Witness literature that had been coming to her house. She said she had been reading their *Awake* magazine, and to her it seemed to make sense. "What do you guys think?" she asked.

The two young men (perhaps well-meaning but misguided) launched into a rapid-fire rebuttal of everything related to the Jehovah's Witnesses. As her youth group friends watched, the speakers did a five-minute "data dump" on the girl, critiquing both the publications and *her* for having read them.

The pastor grew emotional as he ended the story. He said, "Alex, that teen girl was so embarrassed that she left the room crying. The worst part is that the two apologists seemed to show no concern, and they high-fived each other at the end of their talk." I cringed and assured him that this is not an approach to apologetics one would ever encourage.

Several Things to Avoid as You Cultivate Your Apologetics Skills

This story is a reminder that while believers are to use good *argumentation,* those aspiring to defend the gospel should never be *argumentative.* There is an old saying, "An argument to be won should never be more important than a person to be loved." The content should *at least* leave a listener willing to hear more and hopefully be drawn to the Savior.

One's heart should keep pace with the expansion of his intellect. Studying apologetics can enable a person to accumulate important facts and interesting content. One's vocabulary will expand, and soon everyday conversation will include words like *epistemology, evidential,* and *empirical.* The challenges for a good apologist are to remain humble and also to rely on the Holy Spirit's empowerment, not on any assumed intellectual prowess.

Apologetics is not a license to treat people abrasively.

Hours of apologetics preparation is no substitute for prayer (without prayer, a person may be well read, but spiritually powerless).

Apologetics is not a substitute for the sovereign work of the Holy Spirit in the life of unsaved people. (It has been said, "You can't argue someone into heaven." Of course not. But the truths presented to people may be used by the Lord in drawing a person to Himself.)

Intellectual prowess should not be confused with (nor substituted for) spiritual maturity. Speaking of the fruit of the Spirit operative in a Christian's life in Gal 5:23, the verse concludes, "against such things there is no law." This is essentially saying, "You can't argue with that." A skeptic may quibble over some point of content, but when the message is coupled with an authentic and consistently godly life, the witness is hard to refute.

My personal definition of apologetics, fleshed out during these past 20 years of ministry is this: Apologetics refers to content and methodologies which may be used by the Holy Spirit to contribute toward the discipleship and mobilization of believers, and the evangelization of nonbelievers, so that Jesus Christ is exalted and His kingdom expanded.

The ultimate goal of the apologist is to glorify God. On this battlefield of ideas, believers are soldiers, fighting to secure hotly contested territories. The souls of people are in the crossfire, and the apologist works to see as many lives as possible brought to salvation in Christ.

If all of this sounds a little lofty or grandiose, be encouraged by the knowledge that one of the most well-known apologetics verses was written by the apostle Peter. First Peter 3:15—quoted by apologists everywhere—was penned not by Paul, the theologian and philosopher, but by plainspoken Peter, the fisherman. Just like Peter, each believer has a role to play. More than ever before, believers must rise to the challenge of Peter's words and equip a generation of believers to "always be ready."

Alex McFarland
Elmer L. Towns

Chapter 1

Is There Such a Thing as Absolute Truth?

by Alex McFarland

Not long ago I was looking forward to attending a lecture by authors Maggie Gallagher and Robert George. They were to talk about marriage being an institution between one man and one woman. At a dry cleaner that afternoon I struck up a conversation with a young woman, and the talk turned to that evening's lecture. She said she was a Christian, but she did not believe that people should insist on any one, true definition of marriage. "I don't think we should be telling other people what they should do," she said. "What's true for me might not be true for them. We all have our own truths."

I responded, "Really? Can something be true for me but not for you? Can I say I'm Alex McFarland from North Carolina and you insist I'm an aardvark from the Amazonian jungle, and we are both right? Of course not. But this shows the problem with the belief that everyone has his own truths. Both views can't possibly be *true*."

What Is Truth?

The nature or essence of truth is often described as *absolute truth, ultimate truth,* or as our Founding Fathers put it, *self-evident truth.* The biblical view of reality is one in which truth exists, can be known, and is relevant for everyone. Josh McDowell phrases it this way: "That which is true for all people, for all times, for all places."[1] Since truth is related to the character of God, who is eternal and unchanging (Ps 90:2; Mal 3:6; Heb 13:8), the nature of truth is fixed. Truth does not have an expiration date. It is not up for revision or re-invention.

But how does truth work? What makes something true? Three theories are given in answer to these questions: the correspondence theory, the coherence theory, and the pragmatic theory.

The correspondence theory says that truth is what corresponds to the world in the way people experience it. This is a common-sense theory. When a person says, "The city of Indianapolis is in the state of Indiana," that corresponds with the truth that there is indeed a city called Indianapolis in Indiana. That is the easy part. But sometimes a person claims something that might seem to be true but might be difficult to correspond to the world as it is perceived. Someone may say, "This oar is straight," but then when he puts it halfway in the water it suddenly looks crooked. So is it straight or crooked? Is the statement "This oar is straight" a *true* statement? Yes, it is, because we understand through the science of optics that the image of the oar in the water is refracted so that it just *looks* crooked even though the oar remains straight. The water does not bend the oar; the water acts as a lens of sorts, and the light is bent through this lens so that the oar looks bent.

This might pertain to other things. Someone may look in the distance and say, "A man is walking towards me." But after a few minutes it is obvious that a woman is walking towards him. Because of distance or haze or perhaps poor eyesight, the person misperceived what he was seeing. To say someone might be mistaken about a truth statement does not mean that the truth does not exist. It just means he is mistaken. The statement, "Everyone sees things differently," does not mean there is no truth. It just means that some people are seeing the matter incorrectly. One might say this is X, and another might say it is Y. Still another says it is B, and someone else claims it is A. All four may be wrong, but they cannot all be right. In other words what is A cannot also be *not-A*. What is true cannot also be not true. And what is not true cannot also be true. That is a basic law of logic called the law of noncontradiction. Someone may sincerely believe he has made a true statement when he says this is X when in fact it is A. But according to the correspondence theory of truth, that is not a true statement. Sincerity is not a test of truth. A person can sincerely believe he can fly, but the moment he steps off the edge of the roof, the truth of the law of gravity, which corresponds with reality, combined with his sincerely held belief about his ability to fly, which does *not* correspond to reality, will result in a painful fall.

The next theory is the coherence theory. It says basically that a statement is true if it is logically consistent with other beliefs that are held to be true, and a belief is false if it is inconsistent with or contradicts other beliefs that are held to be true. Truth statements *cohere*—hold together—with other things believed to be true. Gravity exerts an equal force on all objects. So according to the coherence theory of truth as soon as a person lets go of a rock in his hand, gravity will cause it to fall to the earth. And the rock does fall to the earth. This theory has a certain appeal, and in many instances it works. But a person can create in his imagination an entire universe in which many things are true, but do not actually exist. Science-fiction and fantasy literature are full of these universes. For example the creators of the sci-fi series *Star Trek* have been very careful to build a universe in which all its various "truths" are interdependent on other "truths." Yet no United Federation of Planets, or starships, Klingons, or Vulcans exist. But according to a strict reading of the coherence theory of truth, these things are all "true." On a more down-to-earth level, this theory in some ways cannot be contradicted. One can say, "The city of Indianapolis came into existence only one hour ago, complete with the appearance of age, historical records, and memories." According to the coherence theory, this statement is "true," and anything a person does to try to prove that it is not true is easily dealt with by noting that "This building only appears to be old because that's how it was created only one hour ago."

The third theory of truth is the pragmatic theory, sometimes called the functional theory. This means simply that the truth is what works best. A statement is true if it allows a person to interact effectively and efficiently with the world. The less true a belief is, the less it facilitates such interaction. A belief is false if it facilitates no interaction. At face value, people often rely on this theory, whether they realize it or not. It is "true" that heavy stones will fall to the earth when not held up, and this pragmatically allows a person to make sure he is not under them when this happens. But again, stretch the theory a bit, and its problems are evident. People in some ancient cultures believed they should sacrifice human lives to make sure the rains came again in the spring. They would kill a victim, and usually the rains came. Therefore to them it was true that human sacrifice brought the spring rains. But did they? Of course not. This is a classic example of a logical fallacy: *B* follows *A*, therefore *A* caused *B*, even if there's no logical connection between the two. But for those ancients, it was a true statement to say human sacrifice led to spring rains because it *seemed to work*.

So which theory of truth is *true*? They all have elements of truth in them, but they all have problems too, some worse than others. The Christian worldview is the truth because it incorporates all the good elements of each theory while accounting for all the bad. The claims of Christianity correspond to the world as it is experienced and as history states it has been. Christianity holds together in a consistent, coherent explanation of why the world is as it is. And this *works* in the sense that if a person lives by Christianity's truth claims, he will have the easiest time interacting with the world as it is. (This does not mean everything will be *easy*, though, because Jesus Christ promised that believers will have difficulties in this sinful world.)

Points

- Absolute truth not only exists, its existence is self-evident. What is ultimately true is true at all times, in all places, and for all people.
- Relativism is self-defeating, and therefore false.
- Basic logic helps us to recognize and understand the nature of truth. Awareness of truth is knowledge available to all reasonable persons, hidden only if they willfully suppress it.

Counterpoints

- There is no such thing as absolute truth. What's true for me is true for me and what's true for you is true for you. We all have our own truths.

- There is no moral right or wrong. Beliefs about truth and morality are based on personal situations, cultural bias, or on one's religious upbringing.
- Truth is what works. If something works for the greatest good of the majority, then it must be true.

What Happened to Truth?

So what happened to the idea that there was one truth? How do people come to the idea that some things are true for some people but not true for others?

The roots of this thinking go back seven hundred years to the Renaissance. This historical period, which began in Florence, Italy, and spanned roughly three centuries from the 1300s to the late 1500s, was considered a time of rebirth. (In fact that is what *renaissance* means in French.) It was not a rebirth of man, though, but of "the idea of man." It switched positions for God and man; instead of God being the measure of all things, as had been the case since the founding of Christianity, man became the measure.[2] This was the beginning of humanism as a philosophical idea.

Francesco Petrarch (1304–1374), an Italian scholar, is considered the father of humanism.[3] He promoted the idea of the strong, idealistic man and centered his works on man and man's ability. Renaissance humanism is "the broad concern with the study and imitation of classical antiquity which was characteristic of the period and found its expression in scholarship and education and in many other areas, including the arts and sciences."[4] This thought process developed into modern day humanism, with its emphasis on human values and humanity in general.

The late Francis Schaeffer, a Christian scholar, wrote,

These paid men of letters translated Latin, wrote speeches, and acted as secretaries. . . . Their humanism meant, first of all, a veneration for everything ancient and especially the writings of the Greek and Roman age. Although this past age did include the early Christian church, it became increasingly clear that the sort of human autonomy that many of the Renaissance humanists had in mind referred exclusively to the non-Christian Greco-Roman world. Thus Renaissance humanism steadily evolved toward modern humanism—a value system rooted in the belief that man is his own measure, that man is autonomous, totally independent.[5]

Humanism showed the "victory of man." This is seen, for example, in the statue of *David*, completed in 1504 by Michelangelo. This David is supposed to be the David of the Bible, yet he is shown as a strong, handsome man who is obviously not Jewish because he is uncircumcised. This statue of David portrays him as the complete opposite of the young, humble David of the Bible. Most of the art of this time portrayed the same message: "Man will make himself great. Man by himself will tear himself out of nature and free himself from it. Man will be victorious."[6] The humanists were sure that man could solve every problem. "Man starting from himself, tearing himself out of the rock, out of nature, could solve all," Schaeffer wrote. "The humanistic cry was 'I can do what I will; just give me until tomorrow.'"[7]

Eventually, after several hundred years, this idea failed. The optimism of the Renaissance ended in pessimism. For many centuries learned thinkers promised they would deliver the truth, and yet the truth—the truth without God, at least—remained elusive. People finally came to the conclusion that there is no truth. As

Schaeffer wrote, "We could say that we went to Renaissance Florence and found modern man."[8]

Modern man, whether he realizes it or not, is governed in large measure by this pessimism about truth, a philosophy called postmodernism, the belief that there are no absolutes, including no absolute truth. According to postmodern thinking, there is no ultimate truth; people can construct their own "stories" or narratives, and what is true for one person might not be true for another. Truth is relative to individual people, times, and places.

So if truth is relative to each person, each person is then free to do his own thing—the perfect motto of the 1960s and 1970s. The hippies of the sixties preached peace and love, with a generous dose of drugs and illicit sex. Their main belief was, "Do your own thing. If it doesn't hurt anyone and it makes you happy, do it."[9]

Unfortunately many Christians bought into this worldview. As Schaeffer wrote, "As the more Christian-dominated consensus weakened, the majority of people adopted two impoverished values: personal peace and affluence."[10] The dominant ethic was to just be left alone: this was basically the attitude of apathy.

Humanism in the meantime tried to make a comeback. The problem was that humanism had already destroyed everything it hoped to build on. According to Schaeffer humanism—man beginning only from himself—had destroyed the old basis of truth and could find no way to generate with certainty any new truths. In the resulting vacuum the impoverished values of personal peace and affluence had come to stand supreme. And now for the majority of young people, after the passing of the false hopes of drugs as an ideology, the emptiness of the sexual revolution and the failure of politics, what remained? Only apathy. Hope was gone.[11]

This is exemplified in today's dismissive, "Whatever."[12] People do not care anymore about anything so long as it does not hurt them or personally affect them. When asked, "Is something true?" they respond, "*Whatever!*"

Implications of Relativism

Planet earth is fast becoming a "no-truth zone."

Relativism is the death of "true truth," the "extinction of the idea that any particular thing can be known for sure."[13] The denial of absolute truth also has implications for Christianity. Today's denial of absolute truth leads to statements such as these:

- All religions lead to God.
- All religions teach basically the same thing.
- Jesus is one of many great spiritual leaders.
- No such thing as *ultimate* truth exists.
- All beliefs are equally valid.

Sadly, some Christians believe these statements, like the young lady at the dry cleaners who told me, "We all have our own truths."

This relativistic spirit presents challenges for both missions-minded Christians and values-minded parents: How can people be convinced to turn from sin if they cannot be convinced of the true statement that they have sinned? And how can children live according to biblical morals when a relativistic posture seems to be a prerequisite in social, academic, and professional arenas?

Think of the implications of this for preaching the gospel. If there is no actual, absolute truth, or if ultimate truth exists but is *unknowable*, then the Christian's claims about Jesus being the exclusive way to God are fallacious. Equally false (in the mind of many moderns) are the Christian's claims that people are fallen, sinful, in need of salvation, and without Jesus Christ are bound for eternal lostness. Surveys validate the point that when it comes to religious claims, most Americas today are driven by relativism.

Relativism (at least in terms of theology) is the assumption that all beliefs are equally valid. The claim of Christianity that people need Jesus Christ seems ludicrous to people today who are committed to what might be described as absolute subjectivism.

Relativism is a belief system wrapped up in selfishness. What a person wants is no longer held against an objective standard. It becomes his subjective standard, and therefore it is true and right *for him*. But everyone else has his own subjective standard based on what he wants and what is right for him. This may be called *selfism*, the attitude that people are free to approach spirituality on their own terms.

When the truth dies, then so do ethics, because if nothing can be known for sure, then there are no real rights or wrongs. Combine this with selfism, and anything goes. Relativism is no different from having no morality at all.[14] This explains why people can allow society to do things like kill babies and take the lives of people deemed unfit to live. Truth has become what the majority thinks. Truth is no longer based on a firm foundation. Truth is whatever is right at the moment, according to the most people. Frederick Moore Vinson, a former chief justice of the Supreme Court said, "Nothing is more certain in modern society than the principle that there are no absolutes."[15]

A House of Cards

Dogmatic relativism can be exposed as both flimsy and hypocritical. So what can a listener do when his conversation about spiritual things is held hostage by the phrase, "That may be true for you, but not for me"?

First, aside from relativism's inherent logical flaws, one can point out the fact that such platitudes are not livable. No one would remain tolerant of a bank teller who said, "You and your bank statement both say your account contains $5,000. That may be true for you, but it's not true for me." People can talk as if the world is relative, but how they live proves that it is absolute.

Romans 1:18–22 notes that truth exists and describes the destructive end of all who willfully suppress it. But a person does not need a Bible to point out problems with the relativistic worldview. One needs to simply apply common sense. Next time a skeptic argues definitively that truth is relative, the assumptions he is making should be noted. For one thing, if truth does not exist, then by definition his statement is also false. And how can relativists be certain about their position if "truth cannot be known"? Apparently the only one allowed to be dogmatic is the relativist! To reject truth, skeptics must imply the very thing they are denying. This is a self-defeating statement.

God "hardwired" our brains for rational thought. With a little practice, people can become adept at spotting error and defending truth. Culture has become like someone who is insane, someone who cannot adjudicate the real and the unreal. People often make two mistakes when talking about reality. (1) They take certain subject protocols (e.g., history, math, languages) and apply them to other things, or (2) they take a method of one discipline and apply it to all reality.

This is called a category mistake, wrongly attributing certain characteristics of one category to another category. So if someone asked what red sounded like, he would be committing a category mistake because red is a color; it does not have a sound.

Category mistakes lead to a common problem in today's culture, in which preference replaces truth. A preference refers to how someone feels about something, what he wants, such as a color of car or the flavor of ice cream. Examples of truth claims are the content of history, math, science, philosophy, morality, or religion.

Too many people confuse these categories. An example of this is, "You do not like abortion? Then do not have one." Another example is, "We want sexual preference and the right to marry the person we choose." These are expressions of preference. But these are issues of truth. Morality, despite what today's culture would like to make it out to be, is a matter of truth! Few true relativists exist. People do not like it when someone begins messing with their concepts. They will be relativistic up to a point, but then they quickly start telling what they believe is right and wrong.

Why? Because there is something innate in everyone that tells when something is not right. This something is natural law. This is what Christian philosopher J. Budziszewski calls things "we can't not know."[16] Everyone knows innately that some things are wrong, such as lying, stealing, cheating, murdering. The very fact that people, when guilty, try to make excuses for these actions proves that they "cannot not" know them. This is like the crook who flees the scene of the crime; as the police say, fleeing the scene of the crime is proof of guilt. This is because God's law is written on people's hearts, as clearly stated in the Bible:

So, when Gentiles, who do not have the law, instinctively do what the law demands, they are a law to themselves even though they do not have the law. They show that the work of the law is written on their hearts. Their consciences testify in support of this, and their competing thoughts either accuse or excuse them. (Rom 2:14–15)

First Principles of Thought: Laws of Logic

Logic is not invented; it is discovered. Indeed it is part of the created order. Here are a few laws of logic:

The law of noncontradiction: A thing cannot be both *A* and *not-A* at the same time in the same sense. This also means that if something contradicts itself, it cannot be true. Relativism contradicts itself. It states absolutely that there cannot be any absolute truth. But that statement is an absolute truth. Therefore it is self-defeating. It defies the law of noncontradiction.

The law of the excluded middle: A thing is either *A* or *not-A*. It cannot be both. The law gets its name from the construction of the classic logical syllogism, which consists of three terms.

1. All *A* are *B*.
2. *C* is *A*.
3. Therefore *C* is *B*.

Or, more simply:

1. All cats are mammals.
2. Fluffy is a cat.
3. Therefore Fluffy is a mammal.

In the case of an excluded middle, no middle term is needed.

1. Fluffy is a cat.
2. Fluffy is not a cat.

Fluffy cannot be both a cat and not a cat at the same time in the same sense. Something cannot be true and not true at the same time in the same sense. That last qualification—"at the same time in the same sense"—is important. A person can say, "Joe is a man" and mean it in the strict biological sense: a male of the species homo sapiens. But another might say, "Joe is not a man" and mean it in a sociological sense: he is not brave and does not take responsibility for his actions. In this situation it is not a violation of the law of the excluded middle because the word *man* is used in two different senses.

The law of identity: If a thing is *A*, then it is *A*. If it exists, then it exists. If it is true, then it is true. This is self-explanatory, but it pretty much kills any claim that something can be true for one person but not for another.

Conclusion

Instilling a love of truth in the hearts of people is more critical now than ever. The truth that truth exists must be asserted firmly but lovingly. Apologist Peter Kreeft says that "the enemy's battle plan," is lure people into assuming that one's endless spiritual quest is the only actual end. Kreeft theorizes that Satan's approach is, ". . . not just to block the finding (of God), but to block the seeking; not just to get them off right roads and onto wrong roads for a while, but to get them to throw away all their road maps, their principles, their belief in objective truth, especially about good and evil."[17]

First Thessalonians 2:4–6 and Gal 1:10 demand that believers speak the truth! They are not here to tickle people's ears. As J. P. Moreland wrote, "Saint Paul tells us that the church—not the university, the media, or the public schools—is the pillar and support of the truth (1 Tim. 3:15)."[18]

Pilate asked Jesus what is perhaps the ultimate question: "What is truth?" (John 18:38). Five facts about truth that are undeniable are these:

- Undeniable fact one: Truth exists.
- Undeniable fact two: Truth can be known.
- Undeniable fact three: Truth corresponds to reality.
- Undeniable fact four: Truth can be expressed in words.
- Undeniable fact five: Truth is personally relevant.

Content such as what is included in this book is designed to equip hearts and heads to stand up for truth. More than just an intellectual exercise, apologetics approaches the pursuit of truth and love for truth as necessary life skills. An authentic commitment to truth involves both *orthodoxy* (right belief) and *orthopraxy* (right action). A relationship with the One who called Himself *the* truth (John 14:6) must manifest itself in what one believes and how one behaves. Though some in today's culture work hard to suppress the obvious, truth *does* exist.

DISCUSSION QUESTIONS

1. What is truth as we have defined it in this chapter?
2. What are the three main theories of truth and what do they mean?
3. What does the Christian worldview say about absolute truth?
4. What is humanism as we have put it forth in this chapter and what effect did it have on the idea of truth?
5. Why is relativism selfish and how would you defend truth to someone who is putting forth a relativistic belief system?

Endnotes

1. J. McDowell and B. Hostetler, *Right from Wrong* (Nashville: Word, 1994), 17.

2. P. O. Kristeller, *Renaissance Thought: The Classic, Scholastic, and Humanistic Strains* (New York: Harper and Row, 1955), 20–22.

3. C. B. Schmitt, *The Cambridge History of Renaissance Philosophy* (New York: Cambridge University Press, 1988), 127–28.

4. Ibid., 113.

5. F. Schaeffer, *How Should We Then Live?* (Old Tappan, NJ: Revell, 1976; reprint, Wheaton, IL: Crossway, 2005), 60.

6. Ibid., 71.

7. Ibid., 78.

8. Ibid.

9. L. Rollin, *Twentieth-Century Teen Culture by the Decades* (Westport, CT: Greenwood, 1999), 202.

10. Schaeffer, *How Should We Then Live?* 205.

11. Ibid., 210.

12. Rollin, *Twentieth-Century Teen Culture by the Decades*, 310.

13. F. J. Beckwith, *Relativism: Feet Firmly Planted in Mid-Air* (Grand Rapids: Baker, 1998), 19–20.

14. Ibid., 31.

15. P. M. Morley, *The Man in the Mirror* (Grand Rapids: Zondervan, 1997), 59.

16. J. Budziszewski, *What We Can't Not Know* (Dallas: Spence, 2004).

17. P. Kreeft, *How to Win the Culture War* (Downer's Grove, IL: InterVarsity Press, 2002), 61.

18. J. P. Moreland, *Love Your God with All Your Mind* (Colorado Springs: NavPress, 1997), 188.

Chapter 2

How Can I Know There Is a God?

by Alex McFarland

Nothing else causes as much controversy as the topic of God. There are many beliefs about God—about His existence, who He is, what His nature is. This chapter seeks to prove that God does indeed exist and that He is the God of the Bible.

Over the years people have made many attempts to prove the existence of God. Two of them will be addressed in chapter 3: the cosmological argument and the teleological argument.

Briefly, the cosmological argument argues from cause and effect to deduce that there is an ultimate First Cause. For example a meteor streaks across the sky, an effect, and one deduces its cause, an asteroid dislodged from the asteroid belt between Mars and Jupiter and hurtled toward earth. The existence of the asteroid belt is an effect of a cause, the creation of the solar system, which in itself is the effect of a cause, the creation of the Milky Way galaxy, which is an effect of . . . on and on. This chain of cause and effect can go back for a very long time, but it is *not* infinite. It must have a definite beginning, according to the cosmological argument, in a First Cause that itself was not caused—an Unmoved Mover, as Aristotle called it. Some argue that this first cause is God.

A variation of the cosmological argument is the Kalām argument, which argues from the fact that the universe had a definite beginning, so there must have been something that caused that beginning. The scientific theory of the Big Bang, first proposed in the mid-twentieth century, gave extra credence to the Kalām argument. It says that everything that exists today—cabbages, cats, kings, and comets—are all a result of a massive explosion of matter and energy from a single, infinitely dense singularity. People disagree on how long ago that was, but most agree now that that is how the universe sprang into existence. Theists (and simple logic) argue that the singularity from which the universe sprang could not have caused itself; it had to have been caused by a Creator outside of time and space—God. The obvious theological implications of the Big Bang were apparent even as the theory was proposed, as can be seen by its reception by atheistic scientists at the time.

Another proof offered for the existence of God is the teleological argument, from the Greek *telos* ("end"), which suggests that the universe was created with a specific end or purpose in mind. This argument looks at the evident design in the universe and deduces that there must be a designer, God. If a person found a watch in the middle of the field, would he assume it got there simply through the natural processes of wind, rain, and weathering? Clearly the complex arrangement of gears and springs show evidence of deliberate design and manufacture by an intelligent agent, the watchmaker. But not only is the watch complex, its complexity is also specific, what is called specified complexity. After all, a pile of multicolored stones might be complex, but there's no specificity to it, and it could easily be explained by natural forces. But the complexity of the watch is purposeful; each part is assembled in a certain order to complete the watch as a timepiece.

Such specified complexity is seen in nature. The living cell, which at one time was viewed as just a blob of protoplasm, is now seen to be a complex factory with many moving parts that have specific functions that must be done in a specific order for the cell to function. Like a watch, that sort of complexity cannot be the result of random natural forces. The teleological argument says that this is the result of a purposeful designer, God.

Yet another proof for the existence of God is offered in the ontological argument, from the Greek *ontos* ("being"). This argument suggests that God's existence is based on premises that derive from a source other than observation of the world (i.e., from reason alone). Both the cosmological and teleological arguments are a form of a posteriori (after the fact) knowledge, which is dependent on experience or empirical evidence (e.g., "Some cats are fat"). On the other hand a priori (before the fact) knowledge can refer to experience to prove its premise, but it does not rely on it. A priori starts from what is already known from reason (e.g., "A triangle is a three-sided plane figure"). One can look to the world for evidence that a triangle is such, but this is already known from reason alone.

Regarding God, the ontological argument argues from a priori knowledge that one can conceive of a being such as God, so there must be something to it. This idea was first proposed by Anselm (1033–1109), the archbishop of Canterbury. In his *Proslogion*, Anselm claimed to derive the existence of God from the concept of a being of which no greater can be conceived. To prove this, he resorted to the reduction ad absurdum method of reason, taking

the opposite position and reasoning from that to an absurd end—
an illogical end. Anselm reasoned that if such a being failed to
exist, then one could conceive of an even greater being, namely, a
being of which no greater could be conceived and which actually
did exist. But this would be absurd, he said; nothing can be greater
than a being of which no greater can be conceived. So a being of
which no greater can be conceived, that is God, exists. He phased
his argument like this:

> If therefore that than which nothing greater can be con-
> ceived exists in the understanding alone [and not in real-
> ity], then this thing than which nothing greater can be
> conceived is something than that which a greater can be
> conceived. And this is clearly impossible. Therefore, there
> can be no doubt at all that something than which a greater
> cannot be conceived exists in both the understanding and
> in reality.[1]

True, that seems a bit convoluted. But basically Anselm was
saying that one can conceive of an all-powerful being such as God,
but it may still be possible that He does not exist. At the same
time, however, it is possible to conceive of a being even greater
than this concept of God but which really does exist. But this is a
logical absurdity, since one cannot conceive of a being even more
powerful than an all-powerful being of which no greater can exist.
So therefore an all-powerful being such as God exists.

Variations of the ontological argument have floated around
over the centuries, and it was reformulated by Alvin Plantinga,
a professor of philosophy and religion at the University of Notre
Dame.

He phrased it this way:

1. God exists in the understanding but not in reality (assumption for *reduction*).

2. Existence in reality is greater than existence in the understanding alone (premise).

3. A being having all of God's properties plus existence in reality can be conceived (premise).

4. A being having all of God's properties plus existence in reality is greater than God [from points 1 and 2].

5. A being greater than God can be conceived [from points 3 and 4].

6. It is false that a being greater than God can be conceived (from the definition of "God").

7. Hence it is false that God exists in the understanding but not in reality [from points 1, 5 and 6].

8. God exists in the understanding [premise, to which even the fool agrees].

9. Hence God exists in reality [from points 7 and 8].[2]

But Plantinga does not claim this as proof positive for the existence of God. Rather, he said it shows that belief in the existence of God is rational, even if it cannot be proved. He wrote, "Our verdict on these reformulated versions of Anselm's argument must be as follows. They cannot, perhaps, be said to prove or establish their conclusion. But since it is rational to accept their central premise, they do show that it is rational to accept that conclusion."[3]

The ontological argument is actually the weakest of the proposed arguments for God's existence. It suffers from a form of begging the question—assuming the truth of the thing to be proved. Apologists Norman L. Geisler and Winfried Corduan note this and cite the atheistic American philosopher Walter Kaufmann's criticism of the ontological argument.

As Walter Kaufmann argued, "Can we prove God's existence with a valid argument in which God does not appear in any of the premises?" For "clearly, if God does not appear in any of the premises, he will not appear in the conclusion either; if he did, the argument would have to be invalid." That is, logically, the conclusion can be no broader than the premises. If one begins with God in the premises, one has already begged the question. And if one does not begin with God in the premises, there is no logically valid way to come up with God in the conclusion, Kaufmann insists.[4]

Scottish philosopher David Hume (1711–1775), the father of skepticism, also had a rather scathing critique of the ontological argument.

There is an evident absurdity in pretending to demonstrate a matter of fact, or to prove it by any arguments *a priori*. Nothing is demonstrable, unless the contrary implies a contradiction. Nothing, that is distinctly conceivable, implies a contradiction. Whatever we conceive as existent, we can also conceive as nonexistent. There is no being, therefore, whose nonexistence implies a contradiction. Consequently there is no being whose existence is demonstrable.[5]

Hume was an empiricist. He believed that the only things one can know for sure are what he can learn through the senses. He scoffed at *a priori* knowledge. Because one cannot perceive a necessary being through the senses, he reasoned, one therefore cannot prove that such a thing as a necessary being exists. In fact it would never even occur to him, Hume said.

The German philosopher Immanuel Kant (1724–1804) wanted to preserve both rational empiricism and the truth of Christianity. In addressing the ontological argument, Kant said that any knowledge of God is not rational. By this he did not mean it was *irrational*, he meant it is *non*rational. In other words the knowledge of God is not absurd; it is just beyond man's ability to discern through reason. A person cannot know a thing as it is in itself (*noumena*), but only as it appears to man (*phenomena*). He said that just because a person can form a logical proof for God's existence that does not mean that He actually exists. But Kant was a theist. Belief for Him was simply a matter of faith. Faith and reason were incompatible in Kant's mind. In wanting to preserve both rational empiricism and faith, Kant was the first to view faith and reason as separate realms. Reason tells what is true; faith tells what can be believed but not proved. The results of this severing of faith from reason in the problem with truth was discussed in chapter 1 ("Is There Such a Thing as Absolute Truth?").

Being able to conceive of something—or more pertinently of desiring something—is some sort of proof of that something's existence. It is not a slam-dunk proof, but it is good evidence. Belief in supernatural beings and a reality beyond human existence has been present in all cultures during all ages (formal atheism is a fairly recent development). So there must be something to it. C. S. Lewis put it this way:

> Creatures are not born with desires unless satisfaction for those desires exists. A baby feels hunger: well, there is such a thing as food. A duckling wants to swim: well, there is such a thing as water. Men feel sexual desire: well, there is such a thing as sex. If I find in myself a desire which

no experience in this world can satisfy, the most probable explanation is that I was made for another world.[6]

As Augustine put it, people are made for God, and their hearts are restless until they find rest in Him.[7] This universal longing for something not derived from reason or experience is a good starting point explaining the existence of God.

Points

- God—the "Uncaused Cause—caused the universe.
- We may offer sound arguments and proofs for God's existence by reasoning. Because faith and reason work together, belief in God is not a blind leap in the dark.
- There is a difference between *is* and *ought*. This distinction comes from a standard, an objective "moral law," if you will. Human moral awareness is best explained in terms of there being an actual moral Lawgiver, or God.

Counterpoints

- Christians defeat themselves with the "uncaused cause" argument. If everything had to have a cause then who (or what) caused God?
- If evil exists (and it does), then God must not exist. He would not allow His creation to suffer.
- You can't see God. He isn't something you can prove by experience because He isn't physical.

The Moral Argument

Perhaps one of the strongest arguments for the existence of God is the moral argument. The fact that people in all cultures in all times know that they are to do right and not do wrong is evidence of some common standard by which everyone judges things.

Atheists have a hard time explaining the existence of a moral sense. They believe that the universe consists only of matter and energy, what one can observe or measure. But concepts such as right and wrong, justice and injustice cannot be weighed or measured. They exist in a realm beyond the mere physical nature of the universe. Empiricists have a universe of *is:* matter *is*, energy *is*. But they cannot get to an *ought;* a person *ought* do good, he *ought not* do bad. This is the classic *is/ought* dilemma of the pure empiricist. A person cannot get an *ought* from an *is*. There is no logical connection between "John is a man" and "John ought not steal" (or "John ought to tell the truth").

Even some atheist philosophers have recognized that physical or empirical explanations of the universe alone cannot account for the existence of objective morality. J. L. Mackie wrote, "Objective intrinsically prescriptive features (i.e., moral properties), supervening upon natural ones, constitute so odd a cluster of qualities and relations that they are most unlikely to have arisen in the ordinary course of events, without an all-powerful God to create them."[8]

That has not stopped the atheists from trying, though. The usual explanation for the existence of morality is that it is a result of evolution. They say that through a slow process as humans evolved, they developed an instinct for doing good and not doing bad because, according to Darwinian theory, this behavior made us more fit to survive and pass on our genes to future generations. For example the traits that led a certain species of hominids to be honest or fair gave them greater survival advantages because it led the entire species to work cooperatively, while another species that fought over resources and stole food from each other were less fit to survive and eventually died out. The Darwinian would say that whatever it was in the genetic makeup of the first species that allowed it to survive has been passed down, and people now call this "moral behavior."

While this dresses itself up as a scientific theory, there is nothing scientific about it. This idea is shot through with unstated assumptions and, most importantly, it fails two crucial tests: (a) it cannot be independently tested, and (b) it is not falsifiable. In other words, there is no way to test the theory that certain behaviors have been passed down through the generations to make a species more fit to survive. And there is no way to disprove it either. In other words an evolutionary explanation for morality is pseudo-science, not science.

This is a classic "just-so" story, a perfect example of the ad hoc fallacy. A "just-so" story starts from the existence of something and tries to explain how it came to be. There is nothing inherently wrong with this line of reasoning, so long as it is acknowledged as speculative *and* there is an attempt to prove it. In a "just-so" story, though, only certain lines of evidence and inquiry are considered. For example one may believe pancakes come from pancake fairies. So when he finds pancakes on his plate and, despite the skillet in his wife's hand and the bowl of pancake batter by the stove, he says, "I see the pancake fairies have been here."

The British author Rudyard Kipling, perhaps best known for his *Jungle Book* stories, had tremendous fun with "just-so" stories. Examples are "How the Elephant Got His Trunk" and "How the Leopard Got His Spots."[9] He took a fact—elephants have trunks—and concocted fabulously improbable stories for how this came to be. They are fun to read and not meant to be taken seriously, but they are hardly more probable than the evolutionary explanations for the existence of a moral instinct in people. The pancake story is admittedly silly, but it is similar to how evolutionists try to explain the existence of morality. Because they are determined to see everything through the prism of naturalistic evolution, they can see nothing else, even if it is staring them in the face.

Another problem facing the atheist or evolutionist is explaining altruism. Altruism consists of those moral actions in which an individual forgoes a good for himself in order to benefit another— even to the point of sacrificing his life. Mother Teresa is a good example of altruism; she spent her life in poverty in order to serve the poor of Calcutta. A man might put himself in danger, rushing into a burning building in order to save another's life. But altruism presents problems for Darwinianism. Darwin said that evolution requires that those beings most fit for survival pass on their genes, causing that genetic strain to propagate, while those unfit do not pass on their genes and eventually that genetic strain dies out. (Darwinianism is not saying that only the *strong* survive; Darwin said the *fittest*. Small mammals that survived dinosaurs certainly were not the strongest, but they were supposedly the most fit to survive in new environmental conditions.)

With altruism, however, people through moral choice deliberately risk *not* passing on their genes, contrary to what Darwin said evolution would compel them to do. Altruism flies in the face of the Darwinian explanation. Some will try to get around this by saying altruism arose because somehow people know that selfless behavior benefits the species as a whole. However, this is yet another out-of-left-field ad hoc explanation.

Here is an even bigger problem for an evolutionary explanation of morality: if what people call moral behavior is just a product of natural evolution, then there is nothing praiseworthy about it. This is just a behavior, like scratching an itch. And the opposite is even more of a problem for evolutionists. How can immoral behavior be condemned? The person whom one would condemn could simply respond, "Well, I must not have inherited that behavior. It is a natural variant in the population pool." However, how could anyone possibly praise those who at great risk to themselves took a stand on moral grounds, for example Dietrich Bonhoeffer or Martin Luther King Jr.? If they were just behaving according to evolutionary dictates, there is nothing praiseworthy about their actions. This would be akin to praising a cat for being hungry and then eating.

The fact that people have moral instincts, whether they follow them or not, points to something outside themselves, a standard against which actions are to be judged. That standard is God. And unlike the other arguments for the existence of God—the cosmological, teleological, and ontological—the moral argument is the best for pointing people to the God of the Bible. (Each of the other three agreements *by themselves* could just as well lead a person to any god, not necessarily the God of the Bible.)

How does this standard work? Does God command something because it is moral, or is it moral because God commands it? In other words is morality some "thing" out there beyond even God Himself? No, morality is not extrinsic to God; it is intrinsic. In other words the answer to the question is "none of the above." Morality is rooted in God's very nature. When Scripture says God cannot lie, it does not mean that through superior willpower God resists the urge to lie. No, God is incapable of lying because that would violate His very essence. Just as a male cannot cease to be a human male, so God cannot cease to be God.

Because people are created in God's image (Gen 1:26), they share certain attributes with Him, among them a sense of when they are in harmony with His essence and when they are not. When a person lies, cheats, steals, or murders, he is acting contrary to God's nature, and he knows it, even if only at some basic, instinctive level. He knows deep in his being that he is to do right (what is in accord with God's nature) and not to do wrong (what is not in accord with God's nature). But because people are finite beings and do not share *all* of God's attributes, particularly His holiness, they are capable of missing the mark—which is one definition of sin.

Some respond, however, that this cannot be true, since all morality is relative. Every culture seems to have things that they consider right that others consider wrong, and vice versa. This would seem to be a fatal blow against the morality argument for proof of God's existence. But it is a mistaken objection. What may seem to be different standards of morality among different peoples or cultures, is not different standards of morality, but differences of opinion on how to apply the rules in specific situations.

For example years ago the Inuit people who lived north of the Arctic Circle practiced a form of euthanasia. Once people reached a certain advanced age, they would be put adrift on a ice floe to eventually starve. Today people reading this are horrified, protesting that all human life is sacred. So who is right, the Inuit or everyone else? Actually both the Inuit and others are operating from the same moral principle: preserve human life. But the emphasis is on a different specific course of action. The Inuit believed resources were scarce, and so in order to preserve human life, they had to preserve those resources for the young and those who could still contribute to the tribe. Because there were not enough resources for everyone, they reasoned that if someone had to starve, it would be most beneficial for the whole tribe that those who had lived a full life and could no longer contribute would be starved. People today may protest and say that the Inuit were mistaken in the facts and in applying the moral principle, but they cannot say that the

Inuit were operating from a completely *different* moral principle. They, like everyone else, sought to preserve human life.

Similar reasoning can be applied to most examples of what seems to be different standards of morality. They often come down to a different application of rules or an emphasis on one part of the problem over another. Yet the most basic moral principle is the same. No culture has ever celebrated lying, stealing, or murder. Of course, history is full of lying, thieving murderers. But people tend to want to avoid being called liars, thieves, or murderers. They either deny they did it, or they try to justify their actions. Or they often call it something else. The 9/11 terrorists were murderers, plain and simple, but they did not say, "Yeah, it was murder. So what?" No, they justified it as a religious duty, as commanded by Allah. To them it was not murder because in their hearts they know murder is wrong. People who redefine these acts of lying, stealing, and murdering are in effect "fleeing the scene of the crime" by denying it or redefining it. And as any policeman will state, fleeing the scene of a crime is proof of consciousness of guilt. Certain basic, core truths of morality are common to everyone. At the most basic level people know they we are to do right and not do wrong, even if they tend to disagree about the specific application of the rule. (And that disagreement itself is a result of the fall, mankind's fall into sin, which taints—but does not completely do away with—the image of God in man.)

Such behavior also points to the truth of Scripture and is evidence for the existence of the God of the Bible. As the apostle Paul wrote, "So, when Gentiles, who do not have the law, instinctively do what the law demands, they are a law to themselves even though they do not have the law. They show that the work of the law is written on their hearts. Their consciences testify in support

of this, and their competing thoughts either accuse or excuse them"
(Rom 2:14–15).

Conclusion

Various theories have been offered over the years that attempt to
prove that God exists. The cosmological and teleological arguments are strong, but by themselves they do not compel anyone to
believe in the God of Scripture. The task of Christian apologetics
is to continue the discussion from there to show that the general-
ized god that can be found through those arguments is in fact the
God of Abraham, Isaac, and Jacob, the God of the Bible.

The moral argument is the most compelling and the one that
most directly points toward God. But those who are His should
also remember that beyond such arguments, they can have the
comfort of knowing God exists through their close communion
with Him.

> For you did not receive a spirit of slavery to fall back into
> fear, but you received the Spirit of adoption, by whom we
> cry out, *"Abba, Father!"* . . . In the same way the Spirit also
> joins to help in our weakness, because we do not know
> what to pray for as we should, but the Spirit Himself
> intercedes for us with unspoken groanings. And He who
> searches the hearts knows the Spirit's mind-set, because
> He intercedes for the saints according to the will of God.
> (Rom 8:15,26–27)

DISCUSSION QUESTIONS

1. What is specified complexity and why is it important?
2. What do *a posteriori* and *a priori* mean? Which category does the ontological argument fall under?
3. Why is the often called ontological argument a weak argument for God's existence?
4. What is the moral argument? What makes this a very important argument for God's existence?
5. Is morality something apart from God? In other words, is something morally good or bad simply because God says so?

Endnotes

1. Anselem, Proslogion, http://www.angelfire.com/mn2/tisthammerw/rlgnphil/ontological.html (accessed July 15, 2010).

2. See http://plato.stanford.edu/entries/ontological-arguments/#PlaOntArg (accessed July 15, 2010).

3. A. Plantinga, *The Nature of Necessity* (Oxford: Oxford University Press, 1974), 221.

4. N. L. Geisler and Winfried Corduan, *Philosophy of Religion* (Eugene, OR: Wipf and Stock, 1988), 81.

5. D. Hume, "Dialogues Concerning Natural Religion, Part IX," in *The Cosmological Arguments*, ed. Donald R. Burrill (Garden City, NY: Anchor, 1967), 85–86.

6. C. S. Lewis, *Mere Christianity* (San Francisco: HarperSanFrancisco, 2001), 136-37.

7. Augustine, *Confessions* (accessed July 15, 2010).

8. J. L. Mackie, *The Miracle of Theism: Arguments for and against the Existence of God* (Oxford: Oxford University Press, 1983), 115.

9. R. Kipling, *The Jungle Book*, www.classicshorts.com/stories/techhome (accessed July 15, 2010).

Chapter 3

Where Did the Universe Come From?

by Alex McFarland

W hy is there something rather than nothing? Where did that something come from? These are the most basic questions of philosophy and theology.

These lead to other questions. Where does morality come from? Why should we/anyone do good and not do bad?

The philosopher Immanuel Kant said, "Two things fill the mind with awe, the oftener and more steadily we reflect on them: The starry heavens above me and the moral law within me."

This leads to the ultimate question, do the facts as best understood lead to the conclusion that there is a supernatural Creator—God? By God is meant a being who is the personal, immaterial, timeless cause of the universe, the Designer and Sustainer of the universe and the ground of moral reality. Christians believe that the existence of God is a reasonable inference, defensible based on these four features of reality:

- The coming into existence of the universe
- The current existence of the universe
- Design in the universe
- Moral reality

Points

- Our finite universe was created by an infinite Being out of nothing.
- The universe is not uncaused, and couldn't have "caused itself." The universe had a beginning, and therefore must have had a Cause for its existence.
- The design of the universe points to a Designer. Creative order and beauty (such as we associate with great art) does not come about by randomly splashing blobs of paint against a wall. In a similar way, the order and design of the universe point to an intelligent Creator—someone who could create complex beings such as you the reader.

Counterpoints

- The universe came to exist by Darwinian evolution, not through an intelligent designer. There are no scientifically legitimate reasons to reject evolution.
- Intelligent Design is not a good argument because it is not science because it is not testable, does not use an observable entity, and is not predictable.
- Even some Christians prefer to keep faith and science separate, because we all know that the Bible is not a science book.

Where Did It All Come From?

First, is the point of the coming into existence of the universe. The first such explanation is known as the cosmological argument. Basically this says that all effects must have a cause. The ball rolls across the grass—an effect. The cause? John kicked it. The book falls to the floor. The cause? Mary dropped it.

Early philosophers such as Aristotle looked at the world and saw it was full of effects. The bird flies across the sky. The bird was caused by its mother hatching an egg. The mother hatched the egg because she laid it—on and on, reason back from effects to causes, looking ever backward to what must be a first cause. Aristotle called this the First Cause, the Unmoved Mover.

Of course one can then ask what caused the First Cause. But that is asking the wrong question. Remember, every *effect* has a cause. But a First Cause is, well . . . a *cause*, not an *effect*. Still, this does present a problem that in logic is called "special pleading"— basically, asking for a special rule for your argument for it to work. Addressing the special-pleading argument is beyond the scope of this chapter, but suffice to say that that is not necessary anyway, because there is another form of the cosmological argument called the Kalām argument.

This argument seeks to demonstrate that the universe came into existence a finite time ago and thus needs a cause to explain its coming into existence. The medieval theologian, jurist, and philosopher Al Ghazli succinctly formulated this argument, though it has been popularized in recent years by the Christian philosopher William Lane Craig, who formulates the argument this way:

- The universe began to exist.
- Whatever begins to exist has a cause for its existence.
- Therefore the universe has a cause for its existence.

In defense of the first premise, both scientific and philosophical evidence point to the fact that the universe began to exist a finite time ago. Scientific evidence for the beginning of the universe include (a) the expanding universe, (b) the second law of thermodynamics, and (c) the Big Bang theory.

The philosophical evidence for the beginning of the universe, includes the impossibility of traversing an actual infinite length of time, and the impossibility of the past being infinite, because of the impossibility of traversing an actual infinite length of time.

In maintaining the evidence for the expanding universe scientists maintain that every object in the universe is moving away from every other object. Thus space itself is expanding. Physicist George Gamow says, "The entire space of the universe, populated by billions of galaxies, is in a state of rapid expansion, with its members flying away from one another at high speed."[1]

This was first posited by Edwin Hubble (1889–1953), an American astronomer who is the namesake of today's Hubble Deep Space Telescope. Hubble was the first to demonstrate the existence of galaxies outside the Milky Way. And by studying the Doppler Shift of light, sometimes called "red shift," he also proposed that all the galaxies were moving away from each other at incredible speeds. (Most people know of the Doppler effect more as it pertains to sound. The sound of a moving train, for example, changes pitch from when it is moving toward someone to when it is moving away. This is called the Doppler Shift. The same is true of light; its wavelength is different when it is moving toward someone from when it is moving away, although scientific equipment would be needed to measure it.) Noting Hubble's idea, Albert Einstein observed, "Hubble's discovery, can, therefore, be considered to some extent as a confirmation of the theory [of an expansion of space]."[2]

This was a big change for the scientific world. Until Hubble's proposal, people believed the universe was essentially stable and unmoving. Astronomer Stephen Hawking said, "The old idea of an essentially unchanging universe that could have existed, and could continue to exist, forever was replaced by the notion of a dynamic, expanding universe that seemed to have begun a finite time ago, and that might end at a finite time in the future."[3]

Some say the universe could have been expanding from eternity; in other words it did not have a beginning. But this is mathematically impossible, because otherwise the universe would be infinitely dispersed, which it is not. Therefore the universe began to exist a finite time ago.

The second reason the universe had a beginning is the second law of thermodynamics, which states that all closed systems will tend toward a state of maximum disorder, or *entropy*. In a closed system the amount of energy available to do work decreases and becomes uniform. This amounts to saying that the universe is winding down.[4] In thinking of a large clock, the clockmaker expends energy to wind up the clock, and that energy is stored in the spring. As the energy is slowly released, powering the clock, it is not replaced, and eventually it completely runs out—unless the clock maker breaks into the closed system of the clock and puts in more energy in the form of winding it up. But left to itself, the closed system of the clock will eventually run out of energy and stop ticking.

The implications of the second law of thermodynamics are considerable. The universe is constantly losing usable energy and never gaining any more. It is only logical to conclude that the universe is not eternal. "The universe had a finite beginning—the moment at which it was at 'zero entropy' (its most ordered possible state). Like a wind-up clock, the universe is winding down, as if at one point it was fully wound up and has been winding down ever since. The question is who wound up the clock?"⁵

The theological implications are obvious. Astronomer Robert Jastrow said, "Theologians generally are delighted with the proof that the universe had a beginning, but astronomers are curiously upset. It turns out that the scientist behaves the way the rest of us do when our beliefs are in conflict with the evidence. . . . The laws of thermodynamics . . . [point] . . . to one conclusion, that the universe had a beginning."⁶

The universe could not have been running down from eternity; otherwise it would have run down by now, which it obviously has not. Therefore the universe began to exist a finite time ago.

The third reason behind the Kalām Argument is the Big Bang theory, the belief that the universe began in a colossal explosion a finite time ago. Scientists maintain that the universe began in a colossal explosion a finite time ago. Physicist Stephen Weinberg says; "In the beginning there was an explosion. Not an explosion like those familiar on Earth. . . . [It was] an explosion which occurred simultaneously everywhere, filling all space from the beginning with every particle of matter rushing apart from every other particle."⁷ Theoretical physicist Paul Davies wrote, "These days most cosmologists and astronomers back the theory that there was indeed a creation . . . when the physical universe burst into existence in an awesome explosion popularly known as the 'Big Bang.' Whether one accepts all the details or not, the essential hypothesis—that there was some sort of creation—seems, from the scientific point of view, compelling."⁸

Hawking agrees. "Almost every one now believes that the universe, and time itself, had a beginning at the Big Bang."⁹

Only one conclusion is evident: The universe had a beginning. As physicist Alexander Vilenkin stated, "It is said that an argument is what convinces reasonable men and a proof is what it takes to convince even an unreasonable man. With the proof now in place, cosmologists can no longer hide behind the possibility of a past-eternal universe. There is no escape, they have to face the problem of a cosmic beginning."[10] Physicist Victor Weisskopf says,

> The question of the origin of the universe is one of the most exciting topics for a scientist to deal with. The origin of the universe can be talked about not only in scientific terms, but also in poetic and spiritual language, an approach that is complimentary to the scientific one. Indeed, the Judeo-Christian tradition ascribes the beginning of the world in a way that is surprisingly similar to the scientific model.[11]

So the universe has not existed from eternity. Therefore the universe began to exist a finite time ago. The implications of this for theology are obvious. Astrophysicist Christopher Isham observed,

> Perhaps the best argument in favor of the thesis that the Big Bang supports theism is the obvious unease with which it is greeted by some atheist physicists. At times this has led to scientific ideas such as continuous creation or an oscillating universe being advanced with a tenacity which so exceeds their intrinsic worth that one can only suspect the operation of psychological forces lying very much deeper than the usual academic desire for a theorist to support his or her theory.[12]

The second part of the syllogism is this: Whatever begins to exist has a cause of its existence.

The argument is not saying, "Everything must have a cause of its existence." The theist's position is that everything that *begins* to exist—that is, every finite, contingent thing—must have a cause of its existence. Everything we now know about the universe suggests that the things in the universe are caused to exist. Thus there must be something that caused it to exist that is itself not part of the universe. The conclusion follows necessarily. The universe has a cause of its existence. But since this is the beginning of the physical, temporal universe itself, then the cause cannot itself be physical or temporal.

Of course, some still might object that whatever caused the Big Bang was itself caused. But even atheist philosopher Quentin Smith is forced to observe that "it belongs analytically to the concept of the cosmological singularity [Big Bang] that it is not the effect of prior physical events. This effectively rules out the idea that the singularity is an effect of some prior natural process.[13]

If the cause of the universe was itself timeless and eternal, this seems the best way to account for why the universe could have come into existence only a finite time ago. In other words the cause itself must not be an impersonal mechanical cause but rather a personal cause that willed the universe to come into existence. If the universe cannot be impersonal and mechanical, then the cause must be personal and volitional—a being who has a will. This is so because if the cause of the universe was merely a "sufficient condition" for the universe, then the effect of the cause would have existed along with the cause.

But we have seen that the scientific evidence points to a beginning of the universe. Thus we have a cause of the universe that is not the universe itself, is nonphysical, is timeless, is supernatural, and is personal. This cause is God.

However, this does not necessarily lead one to conclude that this cause is the God of the Bible. Indeed, the Kalām argument was formulated by Muslims in support of Islamic theology, although the basic principles of the argument are sound and support Christian theology too. And Aristotle, who posited the concept of an Unmoved Mover, was certainly not a Christian, although on this point his reasoning was sound.

So while one can use the cosmological argument to determine that there is something called god, it is up to Christian apologetics to prove that this god is the God of the Bible.

It Is Because It Exists

Yet another variation on the cosmological argument points to the fact of the existence of the universe. Even if someone objects that the universe has always existed, they would still need to posit a cause for its current existing.

This is an argument based on the thinking of the medieval philosopher Thomas Aquinas (1224–1274). When people observe things, they notice that there is a difference between essence and existence. Essence is what something is; existence is whether it is. In other words essence is *what* something is, and existence is *that* something is. Aquinas wrote that when it comes to things whose existence is not part of their essence, it "must be the case that there is something that exists whose essence is its existence." Aquinas said, "All men know this to be God."[14]

The Argument from Design

Another way to observe the universe is its obvious design, which is called the teleological argument. The word *teleological* is derived from the Greek *telos*, meaning "end" or "purpose." Teleology is the supposition that there is purpose or a directive principle in the works and processes of nature.

Perhaps the most famous version of the teleological argument was presented by British philosopher William Paley (1743–1805). He wrote, suppose a person is walking across a field and stubs his foot on a stone. He might ask how the stone got there and conclude not unreasonably that it had been there since the beginning of time. But suppose that a few steps later he comes on a watch laying in the grass. He picks it up and examines it and sees its fine detail and complex inner workings. Would it be reasonable to conclude that, like the stone, it had been there since the beginning of time? Paley wrote, "There must have existed, at some time, and at some place or other, an artificer or artificers, who formed [the watch] for the purpose which we find it actually to answer; who comprehended its construction, and designed its use."[15] In other words, because it is so complex and has an obvious function, it cannot have come into existence by accident. Paley continued, "Every indication of contrivance, every manifestation of design, which existed in the watch, exists in the works of nature; with the difference, on the side of nature, of being greater or more, and that in a degree which exceeds all computation."[16] In other words design is seen as fine-tuning and as information on a far greater scale than is seen in a mere timepiece.

Astronomer Hugh Ross lists more than 35 physical constants or values that are necessary for life. He argues that their simultaneous happening seems so improbable that they could not have come into existence through mere chance. Ross estimates that the probability that the 128 parameters for a life-supporting planet to have come about by chance is about 10 to the negative 166th power.[17]

Physicist and Anglican priest John Polkinghorne argues,

> There seems to be a chance of a revised and revived argument from design . . . appealing to a cosmic planner who has endowed the world with a potentiality implanted

within the delicate balance of the laws of nature themselves, which laws science cannot explain because it assumes them as the basis for its explanation of the process. In short, the claim would be that the universe is indeed . . . the carefully calculated construct of its Creator.[18]

Astronomer Robert Jastrow has noted that the universe was constructed within very narrow limits in such a way that could support life on earth. He refers to the "anthropic principle"—the view that the entire universe is created in such a way as to support mankind (*anthropos*).[19]

Another part of the teleological argument points to design as information. In other words not only does a certain thing seem to be designed, it also communicates information, something that the laws of statistics and probability cannot account for.

Of course some complexity can be explained by natural processes. A person can see order and complexity in a snowflake, but that can be accounted for by known processes of physics and chemistry. But the DNA molecule reveals a complexity that does more: it is *specified* complexity. If someone took the letter tiles from a game of Scrabble and just tossed them into a pile, that pile would be complex but it probably would not form any words or sentences. But if he took those letter tiles and arranged them to spell words, their arrangement is not just complex; it is specified complexity. When each letter is arranged in a specific order to create words, that is specified complexity.

The same is true of the DNA molecule. Not only is it complex, but each part is in a specific place in order to create a specific thing for which that part of the molecule is coded.

Another example is this. A person driving on a country road stops for a break near a large boulder. He notices that the boulder seems to have the letter *A* on it. But examining it more closely, the person deduces that the appearance of the letter *A* comes from natural patterns in the granite in addition to natural weathering from wind and rain. Perhaps a person scratched the letter *A* in the boulder, but based on the evidence, it would not be unreasonable to conclude that natural processes just happened to form a shape that looks like the letter *A*.

But suppose the person sees scratched on the boulder the words "Welcome to Colorado." Not only is this a complex arrangement of letters, but also the letters are complex in a specified way in order to communicate a message. One could examine the boulder to see if any natural patterns in the granite or of weathering might account for this phenomenon. And while one might be able to discern that the letter *C* in Colorado might have been caused by a natural pattern, none of the other letters can. More importantly, the message—a note of welcome to the state of Colorado—cannot be accounted for by natural principles. The letters are clearly the product of an intelligent agent who purposefully scratched those specific shapes that formed letters into a specific order to create words in order to communicate a specific message to anyone seeing it.

So it is with the DNA molecule. According to scientists Charles Thaxton and Walter Bradley, researchers with the Discovery Institute's Center for Science and Culture, "Proponents of an intelligent origin of life note that molecular biology has uncovered an analogy between DNA and language. . . . The genetic code functions exactly like a language code—indeed it is a code. It is a molecular communications system: a sequence of chemical 'letters' stores and transmits the communication in each living cell."[20]

Philosopher of science Stephen Meyer, observed, "At nearly

the same time that computer scientists were beginning to develop machine languages, molecular biologists were discovering that living cells had been using something akin to machine code or software all along."[21]

Even the militant atheist Richard Dawkins admitted, "There is enough information capacity in a single human cell to store the *Encyclopedia Britannica*, all 30 volumes of it, three or four times over."[22]

But Dawkins is then forced to try to explain this as a process of natural selection and random mutation, without director or purpose. Is it rational to relegate this fine-tuning to evolutionary theory? That would be putting the matter backwards. Evolution cannot be responsible for the fine-tuning of the universe since the process of evolution presupposes the fine-tuning in order to work.

Sometimes this is called the "infinite monkey" principle. If a monkey were bashing away on a typewriter for an infinite period of time, he would eventually though randomly end up having typed Shakespeare's *Hamlet*. The weakness of this theorem shows the problem of reasoning about infinity by imagining a vast but finite number, and vice versa. The probability of a monkey typing an exact complete work such as Shakespeare's *Hamlet* is so tiny that the chance of its occurring during the supposed 15 billion years the universe has been in existence is minuscule, but not zero.

Dawkins uses a variation of this. He cites the monkey "bashing away" at the keyboard until it comes on the phrase, "Methinks it is like a weasel" (*Hamlet*, Act 3, Scene 2). Beginning with 28 characters of gibberish, the monkey succeeds in arriving at the "target" sentence in 43 "generations" (separate bashings) on the keyboard, each one moving the monkey closer to the goal. The problem with Dawkins's example here is that the target destination is already known, which presupposes a designer or "watchmaker."

Also the monkey's keyboard bashings are small but definite steps in a *predetermined* direction, which suggest purpose. And according to Dawkins, given enough "generations," the experimenter will always arrive at the target sentence, although the simple laws of logic and statistics show this is nonsense. Most important, though, in order to preserve the doctrine that Darwinian evolution is unguided and without purpose, Dawkins later states, "In real life evolution there is nothing that corresponds to steering towards some distant genetic target."[23] So why use the argument at all?

Biochemist Charles Thaxton, mechanical engineer Walter Bradley, and geochemist Roger L. Olson wrote, "Without a doubt, the atoms and molecules which comprise living cells individually obey the laws of chemistry and physics. The enigma is the origin of so unlikely an organization of these atoms and molecules. . . . It is apparent that 'chance' should be abandoned as an acceptable model for coding of the macromolecules essential in living systems."[24]

Thus it seems clear that a reasonable inference from the evidence of fine-tuning and the origin of life is the deliberate, causal activity of God.

Conclusion

Reasoning from the variations of the cosmological arguments, one can ascertain that the universe came into existence through the deliberate activity of a First Cause, an Unmoved Mover, because logic and reason lead to the conclusion that all the causes seen in the universe—planets moving, birds flying, ice melting, rain falling—can be explained by causes, which themselves are explained by other causes, in a very long but *finite* line back to a First Cause. Christians argue that this First Cause is the God of the Bible, and they use apologetic arguments to make that point.

Reasoning from the teleological argument one can see that the universe has evidence of purpose and design, and its very complexity, including specified complexity like that found in the DNA molecule, point to an intelligent, purposeful force that created them. Again using apologetics, Christians argue that the "purposeful force" is the God of Scripture.

DISCUSSION QUESTIONS

1. What do we, as put forth in this chapter mean by God, or a supernatural Creator?
2. At a basic level, what does the cosmological argument say? What is it arguing for?
3. What is another word for the argument from design? Who was the philosopher that put forth the argument of the watch? What does this prove?
4. What is the anthropic principle as defined by Robert Jastrow? Why is this important to the argument for creation?
5. What is the difference between essence and existence and why is this distinction important?

Endnotes

1. G. Gamow, "Broadening Horizons," in *The World of Physics: A Small Library of the Literature of Physics from Antiquity to the Present* (New York: Simon and Schuster, 1987), 3:259

2. A. Einstein, *Relativity: The Special and the General Theories* (New York: Bonanza, 1961), 131.

3. S. W. Hawking, *A Brief History of Time: From the Big Bang to Black Holes* (Toronto: Bantam, 1988), 33–34.

4. "The Second Law of Thermodynamics," in *The World of Physics: A Small Library of the Literature of Physics from Antiquity to the Present*, 1:734.

5. See http://www.allaboutscience.org/second-law-of-thermody-namics.htm (accessed July 15, 2010).

6. R. Jastrow, *God and the Astronomers* (New York: W. W. Norton and Company, 1978), 16, 111.

7. S. Weinberg, *The First Three Minutes,* rev. ed. (New York: Basic, 1989), 5, cited in L. Strobe, *The Case for a Creator* (Grand Rapids: Zondervan, 2004), 94.

8. P. Davies, *God and the New Physics* (New York: Simon and Schuster, 1984), 10.

9. S. W. Hawking and R. Penrose. *The Nature of Space and Time* (Princeton, NJ: Princeton University Press, 1996), 20.

10. A. Vilenkin, *Many Worlds in One: The Search for Other Universes* (New York: Hill & Wang, 2006), 176.

11. V. F. Weisskopf. "The Origin of the Universe," *American Scientist, 71* (1983), 473–80.

12. C. J. Isham. "Creation of the Universe as a Quantum Process," in *Physics, Philosophy, and Theology,* ed. R. J. Russell, W. R. Stoeger, and G. V. Coyne (Vatican City: Vatican Observatory, 1988), 378, cited in D. Berlinsky, *The Devil's Delusion* (New York: Basic, 2008), 81.

13. Q. Smith, "The Uncaused Beginning of the Universe," in W. L. Craig and Q. Smith, *Theism, Atheism, and Big Bang Cosmology* (Oxford: Clarendon, 1993), 120.

14. T. Aquinas, *Summa Theologica,* vol. 1, translated by the Fathers of the English Dominican Province (New York: Benzinger Brothers: 1848), 17.

15. W. Paley, "Natural Theology," in *The Works of William Paley* (Philadelphia: J. J. Woodward, 1836), 388.

16. Ibid., 390-91.

17. H. Ross, *The Creator and the Cosmos* (Colorado Springs: New Press, 2001), 198.

18. J. Polkinghorne, *Serious Talk: Science and Religion in Dialogue* (Valley Forge, PA: Trinity, 1995), 69–70.

19. R. Jastrow, cited in B. Durbin, "A Scientist Caught Between Two Faiths," *Christianity Today* (August 6, 1982): 17.

20. C. Thaxton and W. Bradley, "Information and the Origin of Life," in *The Creation Hypothesis*, ed. J. P. Moreland (Downers Grove, IL: InterVarsity, 1994), 205.

21. S. C. Meyer, *Signature in the Cell: DNA and the Evidence for Intelligent Design* (New York: Harper Collins, 2009), 110.

22. R. Dawkins, *The Blind Watchmaker: Why the Evidence of Evolution Reveals a Universe without Design* (New York: W. W. Norton, 1996), 115–16.

23. Ibid., 71.

24. C. B. Thaxton, W. L. Bradley, and R. L. Olson, *The Mystery of Life's Origin: Reassessing Current Theories* (New York: Philosophical Library, 1984), 128, 146.

Chapter 4

Is the Bible Reliable?[1]

by Elmer Towns

Just before his death Sir Walter Scott was taken into his library and seated by a large window where he could view the scenery. As he sat there, he called to his son-in-law to "get the book" and read to him. During his lifetime Scott had collected one of the world's largest private libraries, so his son-in-law asked the logical question, "From which book shall I read?" Scott's reply was simple: "There is but one." Scott felt the Bible was superior to all other books for many reasons. Several of these reasons are examined in this chapter.

The Bible is the greatest Book in the world because it is the special revelation of God. It is the greatest in subject matter, has had the greatest influence on lives and nations, and it answers the greatest need in man, namely, salvation.

For many years all kinds of people have held the Bible in high esteem. Yet more recently people have criticized and even ridiculed the Bible. A closer look at the Bible reveals that it is the very Word of God. Many of its greatest critics have never read its pages.

Point

- The Bible is the authoritative word of God in faith and practice because holy men were inspired of God as they wrote the original manuscripts (2 Tim 3:16; 2 Pet 1:21), accurately and without error, and its message is inerrant (without error) and authoritative or trustworthy.

Counterpoint

Some believe the Bible contains stories and messages made up by ancient man and that it has errors and mistakes. They believe the Bible is not relevant for today and does not contain a trustworthy plan of salvation or a workable plan for today's living, but is an irrelevant guide for modern people.

- The Bible has morally objectionable content.
- The Bible has errors and mistakes.
- The Bible has stories and writings that were made up by ancient people or were copied from other ancient manuscripts.
- The critics resort to ridicule to deny the reliability of Scripture.

Is the Bible Reliable?

Some believe the Bible contains stories and messages made up by ancient man and that it has errors and mistakes. They believe the Bible is not relevant for today and does not contain a trustworthy plan of salvation or a workable plan for today's living, but is an irrelevant guide for modern people.

Over 100 years ago the prominent atheist and lecturer Robert Ingersoll attacked the Bible, saying, "The book, called the Bible, is filled with passages equally horrible, unjust and atrocious."[2] Then Ingersoll denied the inspiration of the Scriptures, based on these problems, and he denied the existence of God.

Critics often point to God's commands to Israel to destroy the heathen nations that occupied the land of Canaan. God had promised that land to Israel when He brought them out of Egypt as a nation. Moses commanded, "However, you must not let any living thing survive among the cities of these people the LORD your God is giving you as an inheritance. You must completely destroy them—the Hittite, Amorite, Canaanite, Perizzite, Hivite, and Jebusite–as the Lord your God has commanded you" (Deut 20:16–17).

Critics have referred to this command to discredit Scripture. However, God later explained that He gave this command "so that they won't teach you to do all the detestable things they do for their gods, and you sin against the LORD your God" (Deut 20:18). These nations were already morally and sexually corrupt and would have disintegrated (as other tribes have disappeared from history) by a pandemic originating from their filthy practices (such as the Black Plague in Europe in the Dark Ages) or by other aspects of their lifestyle that were self-destructive. Therefore these nations were under the *indirect* judgment of God (God could have acted *directly* by acts such as severe storms), but here God told His people to drive them out of the land.

If God had not directed His people to eliminate these nations they would have infected God's people physically and spiritually. In fact those nations that were not driven out of the promised land did influence Israel to compromise their faith. Israel began worshipping the gods of those nations left behind (Judg 2:7–13), and then God, being true to His nature, judged Israel (vv. 14–15).

1. *The Bible has errors and mistakes.*

There is a Web page instructing people on how to criticize the Bible, and it instructs people to look for errors in numbering, history, science, and to "criticize the version," meaning a specific translation of the Bible.[3]

Craig James has a blog entitled, "Why Atheists Laugh at the Bible, and Why They Shouldn't."

> Atheist bloggers love to laugh at the Bible, to point out all of its inconsistencies and logical errors. Writers like Hitchens, Harris and Dawkins love all of the horrible stuff in the Bible—the cruel God Yahweh of the Old Testament, the silly mistakes and the glaring inconsistencies of history and even errors of basic philosophy. When you're faced with a Biblical literalist who claims the Bible is 100% correct in every respect, it's hard not to laugh.[4]

Many Web pages point out errors and inconsistencies in the Bible, but there are probably just as many that answer these attacks.[5] Almost every time a Christian answers these attacks, the critics come up with another problem. Perhaps the bottom line is that these critics do not want to believe. The *Bible* calls them "mockers." Then he describes them, "They are deliberately shutting their eyes to a fact that they know very well, that there were, by God's command, heavens in the old days and an earth formed out of the water and surrounded by water" (2 Pet 3:5 *Phillips*). The critics argue that a perfect God should write a perfect Bible. Donald Morgan said, "It should be kept in mind that a perfect and omnipotent God could, should, and likely would see to it that such problems did not exist in a book which s/he had inspired."[6]

Also perhaps the critics point out inconsistencies in the Bible so they can justify their lifestyle or the lifestyle of others. Note the response posted on the website, *11 Things Atheists Criticize about the Bible, but We Know Better.* "The point of the author whose arguments I criticize in the post is that the 11 prohibitions are ridiculous, so the ban on homosexuality is also ridiculous, and we should jettison the Bible completely."[7]

2. *The Bible has stories and writings that were made up by ancient people or were copied from other ancient manuscripts.*

The critics point to some ancient manuscripts to find similar stories to the garden of Eden, or Noah, or Abraham offering his son Isaac on Mount Moriah. However, these stories could simply be similar stories, or the other manuscripts could be copies of the Bible stories.

3. *The critics resort to ridicule to deny the reliability of Scripture.*

In March 2010 the atheist campus group at the University of Texas, San Antonio, began a "Smut for Smut" campaign, calling the Bible *smut.*

> For three days Atheist Agenda members will give students pornographic magazines in exchange for Bibles or other religious texts. Leaders of the Atheist Agenda justify their campaign by arguing that, "Religious books contain violence, spark religious wars, advocate for the mistreatment of women and are therefore no better than pornography" (Atheist Group: Trade Your Bibles in for Porn).[8]

Robert Ingersoll ridiculed those who believe the Bible by claiming, "The inspiration of the Bible depends upon the ignorance of the gentleman who reads it."[9] Then Ingersoll mocked those who believe in the reliability of Scripture. "Is there an intelligent man or woman now in the world who believes in the Garden of Eden story? If you find any man who believes it, strike his forehead and you will hear an echo. Something is for rent.[10]

Others accuse inerrantists of "bibliolatry," that is, of worshipping the Bible. One critic even ridiculed inerrantists for believing in a quadruple God: Father, Son, Holy Spirit, and Scripture. The critic asked, "Did the Bible die for your sins?" Robert Bratcher reflected this view when he spoke before the Christian Life Commission of the Southern Baptist Convention on the topic "Biblical Authority for the Church Today." In part he stated,

> Only willful ignorance or intellectual dishonesty can account for the claim that the Bible is inerrant and infallible. No truth-loving, God-respecting, Christ-honoring believer should be guilty of such heresy. To invest the Bible with qualities of inerrancy and infallibility is to idolatrize [*sic*] it, to transform it into a false God.[11]

On the other hand the following arguments demonstrate that the Bible is from God, and its contents are reliable.

The Bible Is the World of God because . . .

1. The Bible is the Word of God because of the unique revelation of the person of Christ.

The Bible teaches that the person of Christ existed before creation, that He was the Creator, that He manifested Himself in the Old Testament through Christophanies, that He was born of a virgin to enter the world as the God-Man. The Bible declares that Christ lived without sin and died as a substitute for the salvation of sinners. The Bible further declares that Jesus was buried and on the third day arose from the dead and then ascended into heaven where He makes intercession at the right hand of God the Father. Also, the Bible teaches that Jesus Christ shall return to take those who believe in Him to be with Him forever.

This unique revelation of the God-Man demands an examination by any rational person who is seeking the truth. The claims of Jesus Christ are so radical that they cannot be ignored. The claims are so overwhelming that a person must fully accept them or utterly reject them. If Jesus Christ is the Son of God, as He claimed, and if He died for all men, then everyone is obligated to believe in Him. If Jesus Christ is not what He claimed, then people must reject His claim.

The claims of Jesus Christ are quite remarkable when examined thoroughly. Jesus Christ affirmed His deity in several ways. (1) He applied to Himself the words "I am He" (John 8:24). This affirmation is taken from the root word for "Yahweh," "I am who I am" (Exod 3:14; John 4:26; 18:5–6). The Jews did not misunderstand His claim. They knew that Jesus was claiming full deity, and because of that claim, they tried to stone Him (John 8:59). (2) Jesus claimed to be identical with the Father (10:33; 14:9). (3) He asserted His omnipresence (Matt 18:20; John 3:13), omniscience (11:14), and omnipotence (Matt 28:18; John 5:21–23; 6:19). (4) Jesus received and approved of human worship (Matt 14:33; 28:9; John 20:28–29). (5) He forgave sins (Mark 2:5–7, Luke 7:48–50). (6) With several "I am" statements, He identified Himself with God: I am the bread, light, the door, the way, the truth and the life, resurrection and life, (John 6:35; 8:12; 10:9; 11:25; 14:6). Obviously Jesus took Himself seriously. Why? Because He understood who He was. Clearly Jesus claimed to be God and He told others that He is God. C. S. Lewis has correctly pointed out the options.

> I am trying here to prevent anyone saying the really fool-ish thing that people often say about Him: "I'm ready to accept Jesus as a great moral teacher, but I don't accept His claim to be God." That is the one thing we must not say. A man who was merely a man and said the sort of things Jesus said would not be a great moral teacher. He would either be a lunatic—on a level with the man who says he is a poached egg—or he would be the Devil of Hell. You must make your choice. Either this man was, and is, the Son of God: or else a madman or something worse.[12]

Lewis adds that the claims of Jesus Christ must be accepted for what they are: He was God, or He must be rejected.

> You can shut Him up for a fool, you can spit at Him and kill Him as a demon; or you can fall at His feet and call Him Lord and God. But let us not come with any patron-ising nonsense about His being a great human teacher. He has not left that open to us. He did not intend to.[13]

The remarkable teachings of Jesus Christ lead to the following conclusions: Jesus Christ is God, He is the message of the Bible, and the Bible is the Word of God. Josh McDowell has given the chart on page 58 to illustrate this claim about Christ.[14]

The claims of Jesus Christ are so all-encompassing that there is no alternative or middle road. Either a person must believe the message of the Bible or reject it. If he believes the Bible and receives Jesus Christ as his Savior, he will go to heaven, as Jesus promised, but if he rejects the Bible and Jesus he will be punished in hell.

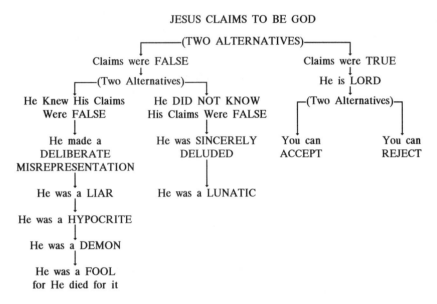

JESUS CLAIMS TO BE GOD

Some claim that Jesus Christ is a creative invention by ancient writers. If man invented Christ, then people face two questions. First, if man invented Christ, why has man not invented a greater god than Jesus Christ? And second, if man invented Christ, why has he not been able to improve on Christ over the years? Since no one has invented a greater "man" than Jesus, and no one has improved on Jesus, the message of Jesus in the Bible must be reliable.

Man would not write the Bible if he could, and man could not write the Bible if he would. That is, people would not write the Bible the way it is written, for in doing so they would have created a message of the perfect Son of God who condemns all men, including themselves. Since God will judge sin, no rational person would write a book that would be self-condemning. Rather, the average man will write a book that reinforces the way he lives. Also, man could not write the Bible if he would. It is impossible for an imperfect human with limited rational ability to conceive of an unlimited God who is all-powerful and eternal.

Lewis S. Chafer, founder and first president of Dallas Theological Seminary, put it this way: "It is not such a book as man would write if he *could*, or could write if he *would*."[15]

2. The Bible is the Word of God because of the extraordinary claims that it is from God.

One cannot prove that the Bible is the Word of God merely by saying, "It claims to be the Word of God." This is a circular argument. Either the Bible is the Word of God (and it must be accepted as from God), or it is the greatest forgery every printed (and must be rejected). The Bible makes significant claims about the source of its message. More than 1,900 times in Scripture the authors claimed their message was from God. Expressions such as "Thus says the Lord" appear approximately 500 times in the Pentateuch and more than 1,200 times in the prophets.

The expressions "Thus saith the LORD" and "The word of the Lord came to . . ." are among the strongest arguments for accepting the Bible. Concerning the expression "the Word of the Lord" B. B. Warfield writes that it "is at once the simplest and the most colorless designation of a Divine communication." He then adds, "Both phrases ['Word of the Lord' and 'Law of the Lord'] are used for any Divine communication of whatever extent; and both came to be employed to express the entire body of Divine revelation, conceived as a unitary whole . . . and both passed into the NT with these implications."[16]

If God wrote a book, His truthfulness would demand that He claim to be its author. Therefore in phrases such as "The word of the Lord came to me" or "The mouth of the Lord has spoken" God is claiming authorship of the Bible. Human authors usually add their names to the title pages of their books. Similarly so that man could not mistake its source, God has placed His autograph throughout the Scriptures in thousands of places.

The uniqueness of the message of the Bible demands a unique avenue of communication. Since the message demands credibility so it can be accepted, God must communicate the message in a way that guarantees its reliability. Therefore in the Bible God gave His message and human messengers communicated that message from God.

Either the Bible is the Word of God, or it must be rejected as a hoax or a fraud. If it is a fraud, people should reject it completely for its lack of integrity and reliability. On the other hand if the Bible is God's Book, its message must be accepted and people must respond accordingly.

The world has attempted to minimize the Bible by stating, "It is a good book, but full of errors." But if the Bible has errors (in the original manuscripts), it cannot be trusted and should be rejected. If the Bible was written to deceive its readers, it could not be from God, who claims to be the truth.

3. The Bible is the Word of God because of the empirical evidence of the fulfillment of prophecy.

The strongest empirical argument that the Bible is the Word of God is based on its predictions of the future. Man does not have knowledge of the future. Only God has that knowledge. Therefore if one can accurately predict the future, He must be God, or receive his knowledge from God, and the truthfulness of fulfilled prophecy must be accepted. Christianity is the only religion that includes fulfilled prophecy as one of its bases for credibility. When the writers of Scripture predicted the future and then their predictions were fulfilled, the credibility of their claims to speak for God became evident. Wilbur Smith said the following of fulfilled prophecy.

> A man who has read several thousand books concludes that, whatever one may think of the authority of the message presented in the book we call the Bible, there is worldwide agreement that in more ways than one it is the most remarkable volume that has ever been produced in these some five thousand years of writing on the part of the human race.
>
> Mohammedanism cannot point to any prophecies of the coming of Mohammed uttered hundreds of years before his birth. Neither can the founders of any cult in this country rightly identify any ancient text specifically foretelling their appearance.[17]

The enemies of Scripture usually do not attack the fact of fulfilled prophecy. They usually try to explain it away. First, they say that prophecies record historical events; they do this by moving the dates. They try to claim that a "fulfillment" did not follow prophecy, but that instead the stated prediction came after the event, and they call it history. This would be a deceitful way of writing history. Another attempt to explain away prophecy is to "spiritualize" the predictions and their fulfillments. For example they say the prophecy that Israel will return to Palestine and reoccupy Jerusalem refers to dead saints occupying "spiritual" Jerusalem, that is, heaven. They try to make words mean something other than what the authors originally wrote.

A British Deist once said that a man named Jesus Christ read the Old Testament prophecies concerning the Messiah and then went out and attempted to fulfill them. If this Deist were correct, Jesus Christ was a lunatic for dying to prove predictions He knew were not true.

As stated, some say that certain Old Testament prophets wrote after the events happened. But the Septuagint and the Dead Sea Scrolls indicate that the Bible books of prophecy were written before the events they predicted. Daniel correctly predicted the coming of the world conqueror from Greece (Alexander the Great), followed by the world domination by Rome. David predicted these events before they transpired. The Dead Sea Scrolls reveal that the Hebrew text of the Old Testament was written and collected before Christ was born. These Dead Sea Scrolls predict Jesus' virgin birth, the place of His birth, His betrayal, His death, and the facts that He was spat on, pierced, and His bones were not broken.

Most remarkable prophecies are yet to be fulfilled. Some have estimated that approximately 75 percent of biblical prophecy has yet to be fulfilled. This involves the second coming of Christ, the Great Tribulation, the millennium, and judgments by God. Though these prophecies cannot be used to prove exclusively that the Bible is the Word of God, the credibility of past fulfilled prophecy should indicate that the prophecies of future events will be fulfilled.

4. The Bible is the Word of God because of the convicting, convincing, converting power of the message.

Even though the Bible tells of adultery and sexual immorality, the Bible is not found in houses of prostitution or places of immorality. Even though the Bible tells of men getting drunk, the Bible is not found in taverns and nightclubs. The Bible is unique in its call to repentance, in its convicting power to unsettle those who sin, and in its power to convert and transform those who accept its message. The transformation in the lives of those who receive the message of the Bible is another proof that the message is from God.

The Bible has a transforming power to change the lives of individuals. This is an empirical argument that other books cannot claim. Thousands of individuals who have rejected the existence of God have begun reading the Bible for various reasons. As they came in contact with the message of God's Word, they were brought under conviction and accepted its message about Jesus Christ. When they came to know Jesus Christ as their personal Savior, they were converted. Harold Lindsell calls this "the pragmatic test" and suggests its validity is demonstrated in changed lives.

> For two thousand years, the Church of Jesus Christ has manifested before the eyes of an unbelieving world that Jesus Christ does make a difference. Because of Him, thousands of people have lived noble lives. Tens of thousands of people have willingly suffered martyrdom by burning, by torture, and by the axe. Children and grandchildren have followed the faith of their fathers and continued their witness.[18]

The Bible produces a changed life that proves to the person whose life is changed, and to those outside who see the transformed life, that what the Bible promises it delivers.

5. The Bible is the Word of God because of the inexhaustible nature of its revelation.

In a casual reading the Bible is a simple book. It can be understood by children with a minimal amount of teaching. When it is preached, it can be understood by those who are illiterate and without the ability to comprehend the written page. But on the other hand there is such depths in the Word of God that no reader can ever exhaust its contents. Whether a person is reading about the Trinity, the two natures of Christ, or the sovereignty of God, there is an inexhaustible mystery in every doctrine. As sincerely as finite man attempts to understand theology, he encounters the infinity of God; he cannot comprehend every part of its teaching.

At times the infinity of God is seen as a contradiction by those who have not read the Bible carefully. Truth never contradicts itself, but truth can transcend itself, especially when God introduces a higher authority, as when God supernaturally performs a miracle.

The fact that the Bible is unfathomable implies that the Author is infinite in His nature and expression. Yet because God desires to communicate His message to everyone, one can only conclude that He wrote a simple Bible for everyone to understand. Since God is infinite and compassionate, the Bible is easy to be understood and yet at the core of every doctrine is a depth of meaning that reaches beyond man's comprehension.

6. The Bible is the Word of God because of the unity of the message from a vast number of diverse human sources.

The unity of the message of Scripture is an internal argument that has its strongest appeal to those who are familiar with the Bible's content. As a person objectively reads the Bible, he finds a unified *message* that centers in Jesus Christ; a unified *theme*, which is the redemption of mankind through God; and a unified *structure* so that each part of the Bible contributes to the whole. And when a person is finished reading the Bible, he realizes that each book is significant. And the Bible has a literary unity. Even though there are numerous authors, the reader gets the impression that there was one mind that guided the preparation of the entire Bible. As Arthur Pink observes,

> The manner in which the Bible has been produced argues against its unity. The Bible was penned on two continents, written in three languages, and its composition and compilation extended through the slow progress of sixteen centuries. The various parts of the Bible were written at different times and under the most varying circumstances. Parts of it were written in tents, deserts, cities, palaces and dungeons; in times of imminent danger and others in seasons of ecstatic joy. Among its writers were judges, kings, priests, prophets, patriarchs, prime-ministers, herdsmen, scribes, soldiers, physicians and fishermen. Yet despite these varying circumstances, conditions and workmen, the Bible is *one* Book, behind its many parts there is an unmistakable organic unity. It contains *one* system of doctrine, *one* code of ethics, *one* plan of salvation, and *one* rule of faith.[19]

The argument of unity is based on the dual authorship of Scripture. First, human authors wrote Scripture and each book of the Bible is reflective of that author's occupation, vocabulary, style, and cultural background. But the Bible has dual authorship. Each book was written by a human author as he was guided by the Holy Spirit. The human author used the literary tools available to him, such as vocabulary, ability to think rationally, poetical nature, and historical observation, but the other Author, the Holy Spirit, guided the writing of Scripture so that each book was inspired of

God and was written without error or mistake. As such, the Holy Spirit gives unity to the Scriptures, hence supplying a supernatural dimension that proves it is the Word of God.

There were perhaps as many as 40 authors, who wrote the 66 books of the Bible. Some men wrote more books than others, (e.g., the apostle John wrote five New Testament books). Yet in spite of the diversity of authors, there is unity in the Bible, and this reflects its supernatural origin.

The authors wrote the books of the Bible over a span of approximately 1,600 years. Moses began writing around 1440 BC, and John wrote the last book of the Bible around AD 100. The Bible was written over 55 generations, yet there remains a singular unity. Only God who transcends all time could be its source.

Also writers of Scripture had a great diversity of occupations. Because people write out of their background, the Bible writers produced different kinds of books. Yet there is no clash in their points of view. Rather than contradictions, there is a unity in the Bible, pointing to God as its Author. (See chart on page 67.)

Also the Bible was written in different locations stretching over 2,000 miles. Ezekiel wrote in Babylon some 560 miles east of Jerusalem, while Paul composed his final prison epistle in Rome, approximately 1,450 miles west of Jerusalem. Some prophets were sent to the ten northern tribes while other prophets wrote to the southern tribes. Yet this social background did not change the perspective nor destroy the Bible's unity.

If a book is an anthology, a compilation chapters by various authors, the unity of a book may suffer. However, in the Scriptures there is different subject matter, but the Bible's unity is obvious.

Even though the Bible was written by approximately 40 different authors, over 1,600 years, by men from a vast number of occupations, separated by as much as 2,000 miles and covering a vast

The Occupations of the Writers

Moses	Politician
David	Shepherd/King
Samuel	Prophet
Peter	Fisherman
Isaiah	Politician
Luke	Physician
Matthew	Tax collector
Paul	Theologian
Amos	Herdsman
Joshua	Soldier
Job	Businessman
Nehemiah	Butler/cupbearer
Jeremiah	Prophet

number of subjects, its unity is evident in its theme, structure, literary emphasis, and thrust. Any objective reader of the Scriptures should recognize that it is the Word of God.

7. The Bible is the Word of God because of the transcultural appeal of the message.

The Bible has a universal appeal, whether people read it during the first century of the church or in the modern-day twenty-first century. Although over 2,000 years old, the Bible always seems to be up to date and meets the needs of its readers.

The universal appeal extends to all races. Many linguists have pointed out that the "translatableness" of the Bible is another indication that it is a unique book whose Author is God. The Bible's message always comes through clearly when it is translated from one language to another.

The argument for the Bible's universal appeal applies to the rich as well as to the poor. The Bible is found in the bookcases of the rich, as well as on the coffee tables of the poor. Also people of all ages love the Word of God, from children to the elderly. Because God wanted to communicate to all people, in all circumstances, at all periods of time, and at all levels of society, He supernaturally endowed the Bible with His Spirit so that it would have a universal appeal. While not a conclusive argument, this reaffirms the other arguments when taken together.

8. *The Bible is the Word of God because of the unmistakable honesty of the Scriptures.*

When an objective reader is studying the Word of God, he does not get the impression that the writer is holding back on anything. When the authors talk about themselves, they are honest about their personal sins, their national sins, and their failures. They do not give in to their pride and cover up their mistakes, nor do they allow false humility to keep them from deserving their achievements.

The Bible is unmistakably honest in objective statements. If the Bible were "invented" by men, they would have been more respectful in omitting the sins of some of God's people. However, the sins of God's heroes are always included. Usually these great men of God fell at their strongest points. Perhaps God wants people today to take their eyes off others and put their eyes on Him. Also God wants readers to know that everyone is mortal and fallible.

9. *The Bible is the Word of God because of the pragmatic test of experience.*

The world is quick to test any claim that is made by individuals, organizations, or especially by a new product. The Underwriters

1. History	Pentateuch/Historical books
2. Biography	Gospels
3. Hygiene/Holiness	Leviticus
4. Poetry	Psalms
5. Theology	Epistles
6. Prophecy	Isaiah, Jeremiah, Ezehiel, Daniel, Minor Prophets
7. Letters	Paul's Epistles
8. Psychology	Ecclesiastes
9. Genealogy	Chronicles

Laboratory tests the validity of new products before they place their seal of approval on them. Perhaps the greatest test that the Bible is the Word of God is its pragmatic impact on the lives of those who test its conclusions. Those who have a personal experience with Jesus Christ know that the Bible is inspired by the Holy Spirit of God to produce their new life. The child of God who has come to know the Lord Jesus Christ through Scripture has no doubt that the Bible is the Word of God. E. Y. Mullins emphasizes this point:

I have, for me at least, irrefutable evidence of the objective existence of the Person so moving me. When to this personal experience I add that of tens of thousands of living Christians, and an unbroken line of them back to Christ, and when I find in the New Testament a manifold record of like experiences, together with a clear account of the origin and cause of them all, my certainty becomes absolute. One of the most urgent of all duties resting upon modern Christians is to assert with earnest and vigor the certainties of Christian experience.[20]

Because lives have been changed by its message, the claim that the Bible is the Word of God is valid. But could not someone claim that the Qur'an is the Word of God because it changed his life? Josh McDowell raises this question and gives this reply.

> For example, let's say a student comes into the room and says, "Guys, I have a stewed tomato in my right tennis shoe. This tomato has changed my life. It has given me a peace and love and joy that I never experienced before, not only that, but I can now run the 100-yard dash in 10 seconds flat."
>
> It is hard to argue with a student like that if his life backs up what he says (especially if he runs circles around you on the track). A personal testimony is often a subjective argument for the reality of something.
>
> Therefore, don't dismiss a subjective experience as being irrelevant.
>
> There are two questions or tests I apply to a subjective experience. First, what is the objective reality for the subjective experience, and second, how many other people have had the same subjective experience from being related to the objective reality? Let me apply this to the student with the "stewed tomato" in his right tennis shoe.
>
> To the first question he would reply: "A stewed tomato in my right tennis shoe." Then the second question would be put this way: "How many people in this classroom, in this university, in this country and on this continent, etc., have experienced the same love, peace, joy, and increased

track speed as the result [of] a stewed tomato in their right tennis shoe?"

At this point, most of the history students laughed. I didn't blame them, for it was obvious that the answer to the second question was "No one!"

Now I had to apply these same two questions to my own subjective experience:

1. What is the objective reality or basis for my subjective experience—a changed life?

Answer: the Person of Christ and His resurrection.

2. How many others have had this same subjective experience from being related to the objective reality, Jesus Christ?

The evidence is overwhelming . . . that truly millions from all backgrounds, nationalities and professions have seen their lives elevated to new levels of peace and joy by turning their lives over to Christ. Indeed, the professor confirmed this when he said, "I have met scores of people around the world that have been transformed by Christ."[21]

Wrap-up

These nine proofs should demonstrate to the objective reader that the Bible came from God, and that its content are reliable. If a person wants an answer to any of his questions, criticisms, or attacks on the Bible, they are available. If a person begins with the assumption that truth is consistent, then the Scriptures have no inconsistencies or contradictions. If they believe truth is a representation of the actual world, then they will find the Bible is what it represents; it is the Word of God.

Most critics say they have trouble with the Bible, but in fact their problem is with the Author of the Bible. Because humans are self-motivated, they do not want to be accountable or responsible to God, their Creator. Because God has set moral laws for all mankind, they do not want to answer to Him; therefore they attack the medium (the Bible) that informs them of their accountability to God.

What advice can be given to the critics of the Bible? They should be told to look beyond the alleged errors and contradictions they think are in Scripture. They should look to God to whom they are responsible, and get spiritually ready to give an account to Him on the day of judgment. Their problem is not intellectual; their problem is deeper: It is a problem of the heart.

DISCUSSION QUESTIONS

1. Of the nine arguments given to demonstrate that the Bible is reliable, which argument seems to be the most meaningful? Why?

2. Of the nine arguments, which one is the most difficult to defend? Why? What happens when one considers all nine arguments together?

3. Different arguments for the Bible's reliability relate to different individuals who have questions. What was your biggest need or question before you prayed to receive Christ? How did the Bible meet your need?

4. As a Christian grows spiritually, different arguments will probably come to have greater significance for him. Why?

5. Why are some critics so condemning of the Bible, giving so much energy to prove the Bible is wrong? How can a Christian address this problem of the Bible's critics?

Endnotes

1. This chapter is adapted from E. L. Towns, *Theology for Today* (Belmont, CA: Wadsworth/Thomson Learning, 2002). See the following pages for extended information on the revelation of God, 30–42; the inspiration of the Bible, 59–72; and the preservation of the Bible, 73–79.

2. Robert Green Ingersoll, *Positive Atheism's Big List of Robert Ingersoll Quotations,* available at http://www.positiveatheism.org/hist/quotes/ingersoll.htm (accessed August 16, 2010).

3. WiKiHow, *"How to Criticize the Bible,"* available at http://www.google.com/search?hl-en&q-The+religion+virus&as_q-Atheists+Laugh, (accessed August 16, 2010).

4. "Why Atheists Laugh at the Bible, and Why They Shouldn't," *The Religion Virus,* available at http://www.thereligionvirus.com (accessed August 16, 2010).

5. Three Web sites answer questions of Bible inconsistencies: http://www.tektonics.org/lp/morgand03.html; http://www.bringyou.to/apologetics/bible.htm; and http://contenderministries.org/discrepancies/contradictions.php.

6. R. Morgan, comp., *Bible Absurdities,* available at http://www.infidels.org/library/modern/donald_morgan/absurd.html, (accessed August 16, 2010).

7. "11 Things Atheists Criticize about the Bible, but We Know Better," *The GiffMex Articles,* available at http://www.giffmex.org/blog/?p-128 (accessed August 16, 2010).

8. "Porn or Bible? Texas Atheists Offer Free Porn-for-Bible Exchange," Sodahead, available at http://www.sodahead.com/living/porn-or-bible-texas-atheists-offer-free-porn-for-bible-exchange/question-896021 (accessed August 16, 2010).

9. *Positive Atheism's Big List of Robert Ingersoll Quotations,* quoted in J. Green, *The Cassell Dictionary of Cynical Quotations.*

10. Ibid.

11. R. Bratcher, "Biblical Authority for the Church Today," *Christianity Today* (May 29, 1981).

12. C. S. Lewis, *Mere Christianity* (New York: MacMillan, 1952), 40–41.

13. Ibid., 41.

14. J. McDowell, *Evidence That Demands a Verdict* (San Bernardino, CA: Campus Crusade for Christ, 1972), 108.

15. L. S. Chafer, *Systematic Theology* (Dallas: Dallas Seminary Press, 1957), vol. no. 22.

16. B. B. Warfield, "Revelation," in *International Standard Bible Encyclopedia*, ed. James Orr (Grand Rapids: Eerdmans, 1939), 4:2581.

17. W. Smith, *The Incomparable Book* (Minneapolis: Beacon, 1961), 9–10.

18. H. Lindsell, *God's Incomparable Word* (Wheaton, IL: Victor, 1977), 48.

19. A. W. Pink, *The Divine Inspiration of the Bible* (Swengel, PA: Bible Truth Depot, 1917), 85 (italic his).

20. E. Y. Mullins, *Why Is Christianity True?* (Chicago: Christian Culture, 1905), 294–95.

21. McDowell, *Evidence That Demands a Verdict*, 339–40.

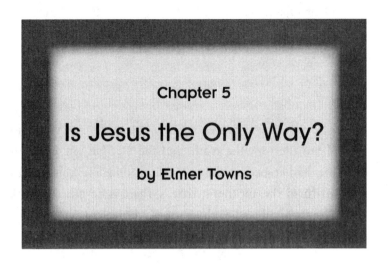

Chapter 5

Is Jesus the Only Way?

by Elmer Towns

Senator Barack Obama, the then Democratic presidential hopeful, was speaking at a meeting at Saddleback Church on August 17, 2008. He was asked the question by megachurch pastor, Rick Warren, "Is Jesus the only way to heaven?"[1] Before this, in a 2004 interview with Cathleen Falsani, who asked the same question, Obama gave the answer, "I believe that there are many paths to the same place. . . . All people of faith—Christians, Jews, Muslims, animists, everyone knows the same God."[2]

Earlier at a town hall meeting in Greensboro, North Carolina, while answering a question about his Christian faith, Obama said he believes that Jesus Christ died for his sins and through God's grace and mercy he could have "everlasting life."[3] However, in this interchange Obama also said that he "believes Jews and Muslims and non-believers who live moral lives are as much 'children of God' as he is."[4]

President Obama seems to be taking both sides to the question, "Is Jesus the only way?" probably the way many Americans might answer.

Point

- The only way to heaven is through Jesus Christ, who said, "I am the way, the truth, and the life. No one comes to the Father except through Me" (John 14:6). Jesus also affirmed the antithesis, that is, there is no other possible way that will lead to the Father in heaven.

Counterpoint

- Many outside Christianity have examined other religions and their many expressions of God, and they conclude there are many who deserve heaven because they sincerely worship God. Also since God is loving and all wise, He would not assign people to hell without giving them an opportunity for salvation in this life or after death.

This question of whether Jesus is the exclusive way to heaven has become a "watershed" issue in evangelicalism. Perhaps more than any other attack against Christians, the world seems to paint evangelicals as intolerant, legalistic, and hateful because they believe that Jesus is the only way to heaven.

The Pew Forum reported that about 65 percent of Americans believe that many religions lead to eternal life or heaven.[5] But does the evangelical belief in "exclusive salvation" mean that they are "politically incorrect"?

Many think that if a person disagrees with the current opinion of Americans, he is probably outmoded, out of date, and "out of step." Evangelicals may be out of step with the typical American, but are they out of step with God?

Recently I was talking to a prospective transfer student in Liberty University. This student wanted to come to Liberty because of the many spiritual activities, such as the prayer meetings, worship services, and the humanitarian service teams of students who refurbish city parks, repair run-down houses of the elderly, construct schools, or build churches on the foreign mission field.

This prospective student liked all these things about Liberty, but then he said, "I believe all religions will ultimately lead a person to God."

He added that a person can get to God through Jesus or Buddha, or through praying Hindu mantras. I had difficulty answering the young man because he was so sincere in what he believed. If I said he was wrong, he would feel I was rejecting him as a person. I did not want to argue with him, yet I loved him and had to tell him the truth. If I did not, then my love for God could be questioned.

So let's look first at the arguments many people give to suggest that anyone "sincere" in his beliefs of God will go to heaven.

Why Sincere Believers in God Think They Will Go to Heaven

1. A God of love will show compassion on those who honestly seek Him—from whatever religion—and will not condemn them to hell.

This argument is based on the fact that God is love, and that He will have compassion on all. Some have used these verses to support their position: "The Lord is . . . not willing that any should perish" (2 Pet 3:9 NKJV), and "For God so loved the world" (John 3:16 NKJV).

Some argue that because people are made in the image of God, when they look within their hearts, they will see a God who loves people. So they project the notion that God loves everyone who tries to worship Him in his own "sincere" way.

A woman asked me, "If some Japanese lady worshipped sincerely at her Shinto god shelf, isn't she going to heaven?" The lady added, "If this Japanese lady followed the dictates of her religion, brought sacrifices to her gods, and was true to her conscience, would God send her to hell?" That woman's thinking reflects the basis for all those who believe that "sincere worshippers" for any and all gods is the basis for entering heaven. The Christian answer to her question is, "Is sincerity a valid basis for entering heaven?"

2. A broad interpretation of Scripture allows salvation apart from the exclusive Old Testament offer to Jews and the exclusive New Testament offer through Jesus.

Those who believe this so-called "broad interpretation" point to Micah 6:8. "He has told you men what is good and what it is the LORD requires of you: only to act justly, to love faithfulness, and to walk humbly with your God." Some people say that this verse is the sum of all Old Testament religion, namely, to be true to one's conscience and walk in fellowship with everyone. If this is what the Old Testament teaches, then the "sincere" argument is correct.

Another verse used by those holding the "sincere" argument is John 10:16. "I have other sheep that are not of this fold; I must bring them also." They say "other sheep" means those who honestly seek and worship God outside the Christian fold and that they will be brought to heaven.[6] The problem with this "broad interpretation" of Scripture is that they pick a few verses, and miss much of the rest of Scripture on how to please God.

3. Elementary logic leads to salvation through many religions.

Since there is a Supreme Being whom all religions worship, and since man is seeking God through many different sources and religions, then obviously the Supreme Being would allow Himself to be approached by different means.

However, this argument can be "bent" both ways. Since there is a Supreme Being, would He not dictate the way He wants to be approached? Would not a Supreme Being have a choice on how He is to be approached, and would not the Supreme Being want obedient worshippers to approach Him in His chosen way?

Believers' Defense That They Will Go to Heaven

1. What right does Christianity have to claim it knows the exclusive way to heaven?

Rather than defend their position "sincere worshippers" attack the exclusive Christian position, accusing it of being narrow, intolerant, legalistic, or arrogant. And they express disgust in a view that excludes them.

2. Are not those who claim to have the only way to heaven negative, intolerant, and narrow-minded?

This rebuttal does not answer the argument of evangelicals; instead it attacks their motives. If they can demonstrate that their opponents are not objective about truth, then they can persuade their followers and themselves that there is credibility in their view of salvation.

3. If Jesus is the only way, why would God allow billions in other religions to die in ignorance and go to hell?

The "sincere worshipper" asks, How could a loving God permit anyone to go to hell? Why has God not done something to save them? This is a valid question if taken at face value. But further chapters show that God has given every person who has ever lived sufficient warning (light) so they could be saved if they want salvation. The truth is there is no "sincere worshipper" who honestly seeks God.

4. Since the Bible has so many errors and Christians are wrong on other scientific facts, such as evolution, how can they be right on the idea of exclusive salvation?

Again this argument by the "sincere worshipper" avoids the real issue of the legitimacy of "exclusive worship." If they can demonstrate that the Bible has errors in places, then the Bible, they say, could be wrong in its claims to exclusive salvation. And if Christians are wrong in interpreting other facts, such as evolution, then they could be wrong in interpreting the exclusive doctrine of salvation. This question will be answered in chapter 4 ("Is the Bible Reliable?") where it will be demonstrated that the Bible is the authoritative Word of God, and that the statements of the Bible can be trusted.

"Sincerity" Position Wrap-Up

This chapter has attempted to give an honest presentation of the statements by "sincere worshippers" as to why they believe there are many ways to God, or why they believe that sincere worshippers will go to heaven after death. The next section answers this position and their questions.

Why Christianity Is the Exclusive Way to Heaven

Many who hold the view that "sincere worshippers" will go to heaven are sincere because they love people, and no "right-thinking" person, they say, would want to harm another person or see him suffer.

But the issue is not what humans think or believe. It's what God says in the Bible. The following reasons are pronouncements by God, but they also include logical reasons why God's offer of salvation is exclusive.

1. Because the Bible claims that Jesus is the exclusive way to heaven.

As noted earlier, Jesus said, "I am the way, the truth, and the life. No one comes to the Father except through Me" (John 14:6). No one can get to heaven except through Jesus. Jesus also implied the opposite: that those who do not come through Him will not reach heaven.

In another place the Bible states, "There is salvation in no one else, for there is no other name under heaven given to people by which we must be saved" (Acts 4:12). Peter had preached in the Jewish temple in Jerusalem, offering salvation only through the name of Jesus. Therefore there is no salvation in the names of Buddha, Allah, or any of the many gods mentioned in Hinduism, or the gods of any other religion. The only One who can save a person is Jesus Christ.

Paul wrote that Jesus has an exclusive role in connecting people to God the Father. "For there is one God and one mediator between God and man, a man, Christ Jesus" (1 Tim 2:5). This verse teaches Jesus is the only one who can bridge the gap between God and humankind.

The uniqueness of the gospel is that God saves those who believe in Jesus Christ. As Paul said, "The gospel . . . is God's power for salvation to everyone who believes, first to the Jew, and also to the Greek" (Rom 1:16).

Jesus said, "Enter through the narrow gate. For the gate is wide and the road is broad that leads to destruction, and there are many who go through it" (Matt 7:13). This suggests that there is a very narrow way to get to heaven, and therefore not everyone ends up there. Why then are some people excluded? Because they do not come through the one narrow gate, which is Jesus Christ (John 10:9). They are lost because they followed a broad way that leads to destruction, and many are going that way.

Jesus repeated the exclusiveness of a narrow gate in Matt 7:14. "How narrow is the gate and difficult the road that leads to life, and few find it." Again Jesus noted that His unique way to heaven is found by only a few people, not everyone.

Another suggestion of Jesus' exclusive salvation is found in the parable of the shepherd and the sheep. He said, "I assure you: I am the door of the sheep. All who came before Me are thieves and robbers" (John 10:7–8). This suggests others have come, claiming to offer salvation. Here Jesus was referring primarily to Jewish false prophets or false messiahs who claimed to be the way of God. But implied in Jesus' words are those outside of Judaism, that is, people who offer false ways of salvation. To make sure everyone understood what He meant, Jesus added, "I am the door. If anyone enters by Me, he will be saved" (v. 9).

So what can one assume about those who claim that Jesus is not the only way? Perhaps that person does not understand the exclusive nature of Jesus' offer of salvation, or he has not responded to Jesus Christ.

2. Because rational arguments exclude the validity of other religious claims about salvation.

Suppose you ask three people, "How could I get to Lynchburg, Virginia, to see Elmer Towns?" The first person says, "Stay on this highway; it leads directly to him." The second person says, "No, turn around and go the opposite way. You'll find him in the other direction." The third person says, "Just take any road you want to; let your conscience be your guide and you'll find him." Logic demands you reject the second and third answers because of their contradictory suggestions.

Similarly one can get to heaven only by following Jesus Christ. And only He—and no other—is God. When Jesus said, "The one who has seen Me has seen the Father" (John 14:9), was He not claiming to be God? And when Jesus said, "The Father and I are one" (10:30) was He not claiming to be God?

Jesus was saying, "I am just like the Father."

The Jews listening to Jesus understood exactly what Jesus was saying. "This is why the Jews began trying all the more to kill Him: [because] He was even calling God His own Father, making Himself equal with God" (John 5:18).

Did Jesus manifest the attributes of deity on earth? Did He do miracles? Did He accept worship as God? Did He make lofty platitudes or speeches that only God would make? The answer to these is Yes. And these are claims no other religious leader can make!

So, based on the fact that Jesus claimed to be God, His claims were either illogical, or He lied, or He must be God.

The illogical conclusion says Jesus claimed to be God, but He didn't know what He was saying. If Jesus were illogical, Josh McDowell said, "Jesus is a lunatic,"[7] because He is making claims that a logical person would not make.

Second, if Jesus made these claims and He knew that He wasn't God, but was only pulling the wool over people's eyes, then, according to Josh McDowell, "He's a liar."[8] And if Jesus is a liar, He is not a great wonderful person who founded one of the world's religions. If Jesus is a "liar," then "sincere worshippers" can't get to heaven by following Him.[9]

But, Jesus claimed to be God and He did manifest the attributes of God, so He must be Lord. He did miracles, so He must be the Lord. He accepted the worship of men, so we also must worship Him. He claimed to be the only way to heaven, so we bow to Him as our Lord. He can't be all three . . . lunatic, liar and Lord—the argument *absurdum* demonstrates Jesus is Lord, and the other ways are wrong. Jesus is the exclusive way to heaven.

3. *Because the unique, inclusive plan of Christianity that Jesus died for everyone in the world implies that all other religions and plans of salvation are excluded.*

The purpose of Jesus' death is unique in that He died for all people in the world. That includes people of all races, of all time, no matter where they live on this earth. At the beginning of Jesus' ministry John the Baptist announced, "Here is the Lamb of God, who takes away the sin of the world!" (John 1:29). If Jesus can take away the sin of everyone in the world, are other religions necessary?

Because God loves the whole world, he sent His only Son to die for the world (John 3:16). In His death He satisfied God's wrath against all sin (1 John 2:2); and Jesus reconciled the whole world in His death (2 Cor 5:19). Therefore Jesus is the Savior of the world (John 4:42; 6:33; 12:32,47; 17:2; 1 John 4:9).

Jesus predicted that when He returns, all ethnic groups would eventually have heard the gospel, and would be represented in heaven (Matt 24:14). Heaven will include Christians "from every nation, tribe, people, and language" (Rev 7:9).

The people whom God includes in salvation are the rich, poor, slaves, babies, children, sick, and those marginalized by society (i.e., shepherds, women, demon-possessed, tax collectors, half-breeds, foreigners, and soldiers).

While many religions target only a select group (i.e., intellectuals, mystics, philosophers, or members of one race and/or ethnic groups), the Bible teaches that Jesus died for all, and all can be saved.

Thus the fact that Jesus died for everyone implies that all other religions and plans of salvation are not necessary, and hence are excluded.

4. Because God rules out all other religions, all idolatry (representations of God), and all other claims of salvation.

The God of the Bible demands exclusive worship, and He rules out any alternative form of deity. About Himself God said, "I am Yahweh, that is My name; I will not give My glory to another, or my praise to idols" (Isa 42:8). "No god was formed before Me, and there will be none after Me. I, I am the LORD, and there is no other Savior but Me" (43:10–11). "I am the LORD, and there is no other; there is no God but Me" (45:5).

Imagine God saying the following to idols, demanding that they prove that their claims are valid: "Bring your arguments before Me. Set up one of your idols and let him predict what's going to happen in the future . . . or what happened in the past so that we may think about our past actions, and know how to direct our future lives. Idol, if you are a god, please tell me what the future holds so we can know that you are god. Do something either good or bad that will astound us so we will realize how great you are. You idols are less than nothing. You are worthless. Those who choose you are detestable. Speak to us or listen to us so we can know that you are right. No one has ever heard any speech from you, so you have never proven to anyone that you are god" (based on Isa 41:21–24,26; 42:9; 43:9: 44:7; 45:21; 46:9–11; 48:14).

Since God's offer of salvation is exclusive, one would expect that God would denounce all other religions and representatives of all gods (idols). And in His denunciations, God would demand that they do the things He does. But since these gods of other religions cannot predict the future, they are false.

God calls every person to repent of his rebellious idolatry and turn to Him. "God now commands all people everywhere to repent" (Acts 17:30). People in Thessalonica who became Christians rejected idolatry when they turned to God. "You turned to God from idols to serve the living and true God" (1 Thess 1:9).

If God tolerates other religions, and other claims of god, or if God offered a way to heaven that is valid along with all other religions, then He would be violating His own nature and what He said about other religions.

5. Because the exclusive nature of other religions contradicts the claim that "sincere worshippers" will go to heaven.

Few people who claim there are many ways to heaven have ever looked carefully at Christianity, nor have they looked carefully at all other religions. They have only naively accepted the popular opinion that "all roads lead to heaven." But logic itself, based on the definition of truth that it cannot contradict itself, denies their position.

For example, Buddhism says that entering heaven is to enter Nirvana where the ego is extinguished. But Jesus said, "I will come back and receive you to Myself, so that where I am you may be also" (John 14:3). The Christian in heaven will enjoy fellowship with Jesus; He will not be extinguished. These two destinations are contradictory, so one of them is wrong.

Hinduism says that the true self or soul of each person must be continuously extended from the supreme soul, Brahman. When a person becomes one with Brahman, he is liberated or reincarnated. But Jesus said, "I am the way, the truth, and the life. No one comes to the Father except through Me" (John 14:6). Again these two ways are contradictory.

According to Mormonism for a person to be saved, he must believe that Joseph was a prophet, that Brigham Young was his successor, and that after death every person goes to one of three levels of glory, depending how he lived. But Christian salvation denies any dependence on good works. "For by grace you are saved through faith, and this is not from yourselves; it is God's gift—not from works, so that no one can boast" (Eph 2:8–9).

For salvation Mormonism originally required polygamy (though this was changed later).[10] Hinduism has millions of gods, but none is the same as the gods of Buddhists, or the Allah of Muslims, or any other gods.

Muslims and Jehovah's Witnesses are unitarians (only one God), but each religion denies the other. In fact Muslims see themselves as the only way to heaven (*Qur'an*, 109), and they reject all other ways. Muslims seek to destroy the images or idols that Hindus, Buddhists, and animists worship.

Those who support the "sincere worshippers" theory ignore the fact that other religions are diverse in nature, and that most are exclusive in their offer of salvation. They do not realize their position is wrong because they do not realize the fact that other religions contradict each other.

6. Because the unique claim of the Bible that Jesus was raised from the dead is superior to the lack of resurrection in other major religions.

All other religions are without resurrection, but Jesus claimed that "I am the resurrection" (John 11:25), and believers in Him will be resurrected. "I will raise him up on the last day" (6:44). (See chapter 6 for proofs of Jesus' resurrection.)

All other religions promise deliverance in and through death, but none of them have ever raised a single person from the dead. None of the heads of human religions has been raised from the dead, nor do any of them even make that claim. How is it that other religions rely on their leaders, who have been dead many years, to successfully raise them and millions of others? How is it that the followers of other religions can hope for life after death when their leader has never demonstrated power over death? Since these leaders do not claim to raise themselves nor others, why should anyone put his trust in other religions for life after death?

7. Because no one can love God or come to God while he rejects His Son whom He sent to the earth.

No one can love God or come to God while he rejects His Son whom He sent to the earth. As Jesus said, "If God were your Father, you would love Me, because I came from God and I am here. For I didn't come on My own, but He sent Me" (John 8:42). Jesus also said, "No one knows the Son except the Father, and no one knows the Father except the Son and [anyone] to whom the Son desires to reveal Him" (Matt 11:27). Jesus said again, "Anyone who does not honor the Son does not honor the Father who sent Him" (John 5:23). And He added, "If you knew Me, you would also know My Father" (8:19). And He said the opposite, "The one who hates Me also hates My Father" (15:23).

Jesus was clear that those who reject Him would be punished. "Anyone who believes in Him [Jesus] is not condemned, but anyone who does not believe is already condemned, because he has not believed in the name of the One and Only Son of God" (John 3:18). Jesus explained that those who rejected Him would face the wrath of God. "The one who believes in the Son has eternal life, but the one who refuses to believe in the Son will not see life; instead the wrath of God remains on him" (3:36).

8. Because of the examples of those in other religions who knew they were not saved, but turned to Christianity to be saved.

Jesus told Nicodemus, a ruler of the Jews, that he had to be "born again" to see the kingdom of God (John 3:3–7). Paul, who was a Pharisee and a member of the Sanhedrin, recognized Jesus as his Savior (Acts 9:1–15; Phil 3:3–11). The pagans in Thessalonica turned from their idolatry and believed in Jesus Christ (1 Thess 1:9).

Others whose lifestyle was commendable came to realize that their conduct could not save them. For example an Ethiopian eunuch pursued God as a Gentile, but yet Philip told him he needed to believe in Jesus to be saved (Acts 8:27–39). Cornelius, a Roman centurion, was sincere, and even did good works; but God sent an angel to direct him to contact Paul to come preach the gospel to him. Without the gospel he could not be saved (Acts 10:1–48).

Nowhere do the Scriptures tell of even one person being saved by other religions, nor were they comforted with assurance from other religions, nor did their belief in other religions save them, nor did God ever support or condone other religions. Rather, God said, "There is a way that seems right to a man, but its end is the way to death" (Prov 14:12).

Ravi Zacharias, a Christian apologist, has said,

> If God told people they could reach Him and be saved
> by many different ways, but not by every conceivable way,
> mankind would still object. If every conceivable salva-
> tion brought up by mankind was not acceptable to God,
> then mankind would [say] God [is] intolerant and narrow,
> overly restrictive and unfair for not letting them be saved
> as they desire.[11]

The problem is that people have rebelled against God, and no
matter where the boundary is drawn, man's rebellious nature will
not allow God to draw the line. People want to determine how to
be saved. Yet no matter what God requires, man would reject it.

Wrap-up

An evangelical might ask a sincere worshipper, "Suppose Jesus
were living today and asked you to text a message to Him, or reach
Him on His web address. When Jesus gave you His web address,
your common sense tells you that not just any address will reach
Him. As a matter of fact, even if you miss one letter in His email
address, you would not reach Him." To text-message Jesus, you
must be letter and number perfect. Even those who use a telephone
or text-message a friend realize there is an exclusiveness in communication. Why not exclusiveness in salvation?

DISCUSSION QUESTIONS

1. If God allowed people to go to heaven other than by Jesus, what would be God's basis for forgiving their sins?

2. How good would a person have to be to gain access to heaven?

3. How sincere would a person have to be to gain access to heaven?

4. Would worship of another god, other than Jesus, be a basis for the forgiveness of sins?

5. If people are born with a knowledge of God (Rom 1:18–20), why do some claim that no one knows if there is a God (agnostics), or claim there is no God (atheists)?

6. If people are born with a conscience and have an inborn sense of right and wrong, why do some claim they do not have that sense?

7. If a person has never heard the gospel or of Jesus Christ, on what basis can God keep him out of heaven?

Endnotes

1. R. Warren's Interview with Senators Obama and McCain, Saddleback Civil Forum on the Presidency, August 16, 2008, Saddleback Church, Lake Forest, CA, http://www.thirty-thousand.org/pages/Saddleback_16AUG2008.htm#JC (accessed October 27, 2009). However, incidental interjections by Warren do not appear in the text. It was decided that Warren's follow-up question, "Is Jesus the only way to heaven?" would not appear in the text.

2. C. Falsani, interview with Senator Barack Obama, *Sun Times,* April 5, 2004, http://www.suntimes.com/news/falsani/726619,obamafalsani040504.article (accessed October 27, 2009).

3. J. Riley, "Jesus Christ Not the Only Way to Heaven," *Christian Post,* March 27, 2008, http://www.christianpost.com/

article/20080327/obama-suggests-jesus-christ-not-the-only-way-to-heaven/index.html (accessed October 5, 2009).

4. Ibid.

5. "Many Americans Say Other Faiths Can Lead to Eternal Life," *Pew Forum*, December 18, 2008, http://pewforum.org/docs/?DocID-380 (accessed October 7, 2009).

6. Jesus was not referring to other religions when He mentioned "other sheep." He was referring to the distinction between Old Testament Jews and New Testament Gentiles. This was His prediction of the coming church, that is, that Gentiles in the body of Christ would be the "other sheep" that He would also bring with Him to heaven.

7. J. McDowell, *Evidence That Demands a Verdict* (San Bernardino, CA: Campus Crusade for Christ International, 1972), 108.

8. Ibid.

9. Ibid.

10. "Doctrine and Covenants," 132:1–24; *Journal of Discourses, 11:* 269.

11. R. Zacharias, *Jesus Among Other Gods: The Absolute Claims of the Christian Message* (Nashville: Word, 2000).

Chapter 6

Are the Claims of Jesus' Physical Resurrection from the Dead Valid?

by Alex McFarland

When I was in tenth grade, I had a teacher who was an atheist. It was the first experience I had ever had with an atheist. I grew up in a small farm town in the Bible belt where everyone I knew at least held a belief in God. She was quick to point out that the Bible was no different from any other piece of classic literature and that beliefs in God and Christianity are based on nothing more than fairy tales.

This was the first class in which we had to write a research paper. We were told we could pick any topic. When it was my turn to tell the teacher my topic, I said I chose to write about Jesus' death and resurrection. I had recently been exposed to the book *The Case for Christ*, by Lee Strobel, and was eager to do more research and try to show my teacher why my beliefs were not based on the same thing as a fairy tale. At first she would not allow me to write on that topic, but then she conceded and said I could do my paper on Jesus' death and resurrection only if I could find "real evidence" and not use the Bible. And if not, then she would give me a failing grade, which, given how much weight the paper was worth for our final grade, would cause me to fail not just the paper but the class. I decided to go for it because I was confident that I could find "real evidence" without using the Bible. I was not disappointed. I found a plethora of evidence for the resurrection, and I did not fail the class. The teacher could find nothing wrong with my evidence, and in the end she conceded that maybe there was more to Christianity than myths.

My experience then shows why it is so important that the church know how to defend its beliefs, and how to defend the very important fact of Jesus' resurrection.

The resurrection is the concrete foundation of Christianity. On it sits the rest of Christianity. Without it the entire system of belief will crumble. Defending this key doctrine of Christianity is of utmost importance, that is, if it is true. As the apostle Paul wrote, "If Christ has not been raised, then our preaching is without foundation, and so is your faith. . . . And if Christ has not been raised, your faith is worthless; you are still in your sins" (1 Cor 15:14,17).

Points

- Jesus Christ died on the cross, was buried, and physically arose three days later. His literal resurrection proves that He is the Savior.

- Archeological discoveries have given us reason to accept the historical accuracy of the Bible. We therefore have reason to believe the testimony of those who were eyewitnesses of the risen Jesus.

- The resurrection of Christ is central to Christianity. If Christ did not rise, Christianity is false. Because His resurrection is historically documentable, Christianity is established.

Counterpoints

- The disciples who claimed to see Jesus alive after death may have been hallucinating. We may never know what really happened, but dead bodies simply do not come back from the grave.
- The disciples could have been a bunch of liars! They just made it up. The uneducated people of that time would have accepted the story just as they did other ancient myths.
- To me, the story of Jesus' resurrection sounds like something Christians say just to make their beliefs appear greater than everybody else's.

Five Theories

The Bible clearly teaches that Jesus died on the cross, was buried, and on the third day rose again from the dead and appeared to many people in the coming weeks. In an effort to explain away this most basic teaching of Scripture, people have come up with various explanations.[1] In short, there are five possible accounts: the teaching of Christianity; the disciples hallucinated when they thought they saw the resurrected Christ; the story is just a myth created by early Christians; the resurrection story is a conspiracy concocted by the disciples; and Jesus did not really die—He just swooned and later regained consciousness in the cool of the tomb.

As a matrix, it would look like this:

1.	Jesus died	Jesus rose	Christianity
2.	Jesus died	Jesus did not rise—apostles were deceived	Hallucination
3.	Jesus died	Jesus did not rise—apostles were myth-makers	Myth
4.	Jesus died	Jesus did not rise—apostles were deceivers	Conspiracy
5.	Jesus did not die		Swoon

Deceived or deceivers?

Theories 2 and 4 present a problem: if Jesus did not rise, then the apostles who taught that He did were either deceived (if they thought He did) or deceivers (if they knew He did not).

Blaise Pascal (1623–1662), a French mathematician and philosopher, gave a simple, psychologically sound proof for why any of these explanations is unthinkable. In his *Pensées* (French for *thoughts*), Pascal wrote:

> The apostles were either deceived or deceivers. Either supposition is difficult, for it is not possible to imagine that a man has risen from the dead. While Jesus was with them, he could sustain them; but afterwards, if he did not appear to them, who did make them act? The hypothesis that the apostles were knaves is quite absurd. Follow it out to the end, and imagine these twelve men meeting after Jesus' death and conspiring to say that he has risen from the dead. This means attacking all the powers that be.

The human heart is singularly susceptible to fickleness, to change, to promises, to bribery. One of them had only to deny his story under these inducements, or still more because of possible imprisonment, tortures and death, and they would all have been lost. Follow that out.[2]

The "cruncher" in this argument is the historical fact that no one, weak or strong, saint or sinner, Christian or heretic, ever confessed, freely or under pressure, bribe or even torture, that the story of Jesus' resurrection was a fake, a lie, a deliberate deception. Even when people broke under torture, denied Christ, and worshipped Caesar, they never let *that* cat out of the bag, never revealed that the resurrection was their conspiracy. For that cat was never *in* that bag. No Christians believed Jesus' resurrection was a conspiracy; if they had, they would not have become Christians.[3]

Thomas Aquinas (1224–1274), well-known medieval theologian, had similar thoughts. He wrote:

In the midst of the tyranny of the persecutors, an innumerable throng of people, both simple and learned, flocked to the Christian faith. In this faith there are truths proclaimed that surpass every human intellect; the pleasures of the flesh are curbed; it is taught that the things of the world should be spurned. Now, for the minds of mortal men to assent to these things is the greatest of miracles. . . . This wonderful conversion of the world to the Christian faith is the clearest witness. . . . For it would be truly more wonderful than all signs if the world had been led by simple and humble men to believe such lofty truths, to accomplish such difficult actions, and to have such high hopes.[4]

Think also about the possibility that the disciples knew Jesus was not resurrected but concocted the story for whatever reason. They still had to deal with the issue of the missing body. If they had made up the story, why was the tomb empty?

The Jewish leaders anticipated someone trying to steal Jesus' body, so they persuaded Pontius Pilate to put a seal on the tomb and mount a guard (Matt 27:65–66). The "guard," however, was a group of soldiers in the temple police. (Even today the military term *guard* can mean either a single sentry or an entire guard section of multiple soldiers, depending on the context.) To think that a group of rag-tag Jewish fishermen could have overcome the heavily armed temple guard, break the seal on the tomb, roll away the huge stone, and steal the body of Jesus without anyone else knowing about it defies belief.

This would then mean that the disciples were preaching Christ's resurrection that they knew was a lie. They certainly did not benefit from this lie. They were scattered from their homes and suffered severe persecution, suffering a horrible death (all except John). To believe that they suffered all this, knowing they were defending a lie, again defies belief. True, many people have willingly died for a lie, but the important point is that: they did not know it was a lie! The disciples willingly suffered severe persecution and died horrible deaths. But they could have stopped this at any time simply by confessing that is was a fraud. But it wasn't, and therefore they didn't.

They were just seeing things.

Some might say that the disciples were merely seeing things when they thought they saw the resurrected Christ. The problem is that these hallucinations would explain only the post-Resurrection appearances; they would not explain the empty tomb, the rolled-away stone, or the inability to produce the corpse. No theory can explain all these data except a real resurrection. As C. S. Lewis wrote:

> Any theory of hallucination breaks down on the fact (and if it is invention [rather than fact], it is the oddest invention that ever entered the mind of man) that on three separate occasions this hallucination was not immediately recognized as Jesus (Lk 24:13–31; Jn 20:15; 21:4). Even granting that God sent a holy hallucination to teach truths already widely believed without it, and far more easily taught by other methods, and certain to be completely obscured by this, might we not at least hope that he would get the face of the hallucination *right*? Is he who made all faces such a bungler that he cannot even work up a recognizable likeness of the Man who was himself?[5]

It's just a likeable myth.

Some who respect the "teachings" of Christianity try to soften their objection to Jesus' literal resurrection by saying that the Gospel accounts merely rose as a form of myth over the early years of the church. They say this myth is neither literally true nor literally false, but spiritually or symbolically true. This is the standard line of liberal theology departments in many institutions of higher education throughout the Western world today.

But the Gospel accounts differ drastically from myths. Comparing the Gospels with two particular mythic writings from around that time reveals the stylistic differences. The first is the so-called *Gospel of Peter*, a forgery from around AD 125, which John Dominic Crossan of the "Jesus Seminar," a current media darling among the doubters, insists is earlier than the four Gospels. As William Lane Craig puts it,

In this account, the tomb is not only surrounded by Roman guards but also by all the Jewish Pharisees and elders as well as a great multitude from all the surrounding countryside who have come to watch the resurrection. Suddenly in the night there rings out a loud voice in heaven, and two men descend from heaven to the tomb. The stone over the door rolls back by itself, and they go into the tomb. The three men come out of the tomb, two of them holding up the third man. The heads of the two men reach up into the clouds, but the head of the third man reaches beyond the clouds. Then a cross comes out of the tomb, and a voice from heaven asks, "Have you preached to them that sleep?" And the cross answers, 'Yes.'"[6]

Here is a second comparison, from Richard Purtill:

It may be worthwhile to take a quick look, for purposes of comparison at the closest thing we have around the time of the Gospels to an attempt at a realistic fantasy. This is the story of Apollonius of Tyana, written about AD 250 by Flavius Philostratus. . . . There is some evidence that a neo-Pythagorean sage named Apollonius may really have lived, and thus Philostratus' work is a real example of what some have thought the Gospels to be: a fictionalized account of the life of a real sage and teacher, introducing miraculous elements to build up the prestige of the central figure. It thus gives us a good look at what a real example of a fictionalized biography would look like, written at a time and place not too far removed from those in which the Gospels were written.

The first thing we notice is the fairy-tale atmosphere.

There is a rather nice little vampire story, which inspired a minor poem by Keats entitled *Lamia*. There are animal stories about, for instance, snakes in India big enough to drag off and eat an elephant. The sage wanders from country to country and wherever he goes he is likely to be entertained by the king or emperor, who holds long conversations with him and sends him on his way with camels and precious stones.

Here is a typical passage about healing miracles: "A woman who had had seven miscarriages was cured through the prayers of her husband, as follows. The Wise Man told the husband, when his wife was in labor, to bring a live rabbit under his cloak to the place where she was, walk around her and immediately release the rabbit; for she would lose her womb as well as her baby if the rabbit was not immediately driven away" [Bk 3, sec 39].

The point is that this is what you get when the imagination goes to work. Once the boundaries of fact are crossed we wander into fairyland. And very nice too, for amusement or recreation. But the Gospels are set firmly in the real Palestine of the first century, and the little details are not picturesque inventions but the real details that only an eyewitness or a skilled realistic novelist can give.[7]

William Lane Craig summarizes the evidence, actually the *lack* of evidence:

The Gospels are a miraculous story, and we have no other story handed down to us than that contained in the Gospels. . . . The letters of Barnabas and Clement refer to Jesus' miracles and resurrection. Polycarp mentions the resurrection of Christ, and Irenaeus relates that he had heard Polycarp tell of Jesus' miracles. Ignatius speaks of the resurrection. Puadratus reports that persons were still living who had been healed by Jesus. Justin Martyr mentions the miracles of Christ. No relic of a non-miraculous story exists. That the original story should be lost and replaced by another goes beyond any known example of corruption of even oral tradition, not to speak of the experience of written transmissions. These facts show that the story in the Gospels was in substance the same story that Christians had at the beginning. This means . . . that the resurrection of Jesus was always a part of the story.[8]

Other reasons some do not believe.

A lot of people do not believe in the resurrection, not out of any serious or even nonserious intellectual investigation, but mostly because they are intellectually lazy. They have no sincere desire to know truth. They might also be influenced by a certain strain of antiintellectual Christians who see no need for apologetics and simply say, "Just believe."

A lot of these people are also influenced by the philosophies that came out of the Enlightenment, that period of intellectual ferment in which faith was derided as antiintellectual. Scottish philosopher David Hume (1711–1776), the father of modern skepticism, said that a wise man makes decisions based on greater evidence, and he argued against the possibility of miracles as being without evidence.

But some people disbelieve in miracles no matter what the evidence. Doug Geivett and Gary Habermas note that the reason some people refuse to believe in miracles is that it first requires a belief in God. "For it is not until we notice that the agent responsible for the event must be (or probably is) God that we are in a position to call the event a miracle."[9] But to acknowledge the existence of God brings with it many implications for morality and the way people live, and perhaps even on an unconscious level they refuse to believe because of that.

They add that some naturalists—those who do not believe in the supernatural—claim the resurrection was a one-time event rather "than be forced to come up with a plausible explanation that is compatible with naturalism."[10]

Why you should believe.

But here is some evidence to consider.

Noted apologist Josh McDowell wrote, "Because the New Testament provides the primary historical source for information on the resurrection, many critics during the nineteenth-century attacked the reliability of these biblical documents."[11]

But as McDowell noted, by the end of the nineteenth century archaeological discoveries had confirmed the accuracy of the New Testament manuscripts, and discoveries of early papyri bridged the gap between the time of Christ and existing manuscripts from a later date.

Based on the reliability of Scripture J. Gresham Machen, a twentieth-century theologian at Princeton University, said that the opposition to belief in Jesus' resurrection founders on lack of evidence, not the other way around. He said that not believing in His resurrection might be warranted if one were just talking about a first-century man, otherwise unknown, who rose from the dead. But, he continued, "As a matter of fact the question is not whether any ordinary man rose from the dead, but whether Jesus rose from the dead. We know something of Jesus from the Gospels, and as thus made known He is certainly different from all other men. . . .

Thus when the extraordinary testimony to the resurrection faith . . . comes to us, we add to this our tremendous impression of Jesus' person, gained from the reading of the Gospels, and we accept this strange belief which comes to us and fills us with joy, that the Redeemer really triumphed over death and the grave and sin."[12]

There are other factual, evidential reasons to believe in the resurrection. Burial in tombs hewn out of solid stone was a common fact in the Jerusalem of Jesus' day. In fact many of them can still be seen today. Jesus was buried in the tomb of a member of the Sanhedrin, in accord with the prophecy in Isa 53:9, "They made His grave with the wicked, and with a rich man at His death." That member of the Sanhedrin was specifically named: Joseph of Arimathea. This historical detail is important, because knowing the hostility of the Jews, it is unlikely that they would merely make up a name.

First Corinthians 15:3–5 also reveals that the teaching of Jesus' resurrection was part of a very early creed of the church, and for evidence the apostle Paul specifically cited numerous eyewitnesses to the resurrection (vv. 5–8).

Why It Matters

Aside from being a basic doctrine of Christianity, several implications are to be noted if Christ did not rise from the grave. In a sermon preached in the chapel of Princeton Seminary in the early part of the twentieth century, theologian Benjamin B. Warfield said that people today do not need the resurrection to believe in Christ's love; after all, He died for everyone. One could even believe in His triumph over evil. But with the resurrection

> we have the assurance that He [Jesus] is the Lord of heaven and earth whose right it is to rule and in whose hands are gathered the reins of the universe. . . . [H]ad

he not risen, could we believe Him enthroned in heaven, Lord of all? Himself subject to death; Himself the helpless prisoner of the grave; does He differ in kind from that endless procession of the slaves of death journeying like Him through the world to the one inevitable end?[13]

Fundamental to Christianity is the fact that Jesus should be Lord of all, Warfield said. It is essential that everything be subject to Him, including death.

This last enemy too He must needs . . . put under His feet; and it is because He has put this last enemy under His feet that we can say with such energy of conviction that nothing can separate us from the love of God which is in Christ Jesus our Lord, not even death itself: and that nothing can harm us and nothing take away our peace.[14]

In other words without Jesus' resurrection no one has any assurance the Christ is Lord of *all* things, including death and the grave. With the knowledge that He has triumphed even over those, believers have assurance of His sovereignty. Also one's eternal security rests on the fact Jesus rose from the dead. As John MacArthur says, "All gospel realities hinge on His resurrection, and your eternity is at stake."[15]

DISCUSSION QUESTIONS

1. Why is the resurrection so central to Christianity? What may we conclude about Christianity if the resurrection had not taken place?

2. What are the five naturalistic theories commonly used to explain the resurrection?

3. If the disciples and believers had fabricated the resurrection story they could have admitted this and avoided torture and persecution. Why is this fact important to the argument for belief in the resurrection?

4. Name at least one other objection against the resurrection apart from the five naturalistic theories? How would you try to convince a person whose objection(s) weren't based on these theories

5. What are two proofs for the historicity of Jesus' resurrection? How is the resurrection an example of faith and reason joined together? Why is it important to have a firm foundation for your beliefs?

Endnotes

1. P. Kreeft and R. K. Tacelli, *Handbook of Christian Apologetics* (Grand Rapids: InterVarsity, 1994), 181–95.

2. B. Pascal, *Pensées*, trans. W. F. Trotter (New York: Sutton, 1958), 322, 310.

3. Kreeft and Tacelli, *Handbook of Christian Apologetics*, 185.

4. T. Aquinas, *Summa Theologica* (Notre Dame, IN: Christian Classics, 1980), Q. 3, article 4, 1:17.

5. C. S. Lewis, *Miracles* (reprint, San Francisco: HarperOne, 2001), 241.

6. W. L. Craig, *Apologetics* (Chicago: Moody, 1989), 189.

7. R. Purtill, *Thinking about Religion: A Philosophical Introduction to Religion* (New York: Prentice Hall, 1978), 75–76.

8. W. L. Craig, cited in Kreeft and Tacelli, *Handbook of Christian Apologetics*, 192.

9. D. Geivett and G. Habermas, *In Defense of Miracles* (Downers Grove, IL: InterVarsity, 1997), 181.

10. Ibid.

11. J. McDowell, *Evidence that Demands a Verdict*, http://www.lead-eru.com/everystudent/easter/articles/josh2.html.

12. J. G. Machen, "The Resurrection of Christ," *Reformation Ink*, http://web.archive.org/web/20031019001131/homepage.mac.com/shan-erosenthal/reformationink/jgmresurrection.htm (accessed July 2010).

13. B. B. Warfield, http://homepage.mac.com/shanerosenthal/ref-ormationink/bbwrisenjesus.htm (accessed July 2010).

14. Ibid.

15. J. F. MacArthur, "Resurrection: The Key to Everything," http://www.ondoctrine.com/2mac0058.htm (accessed July 2010).

Chapter 7

Are the Heathen Really Lost?

by Elmer Towns

I settled into my coach sent for a flight out of Lynchburg. A businessman buckled himself into the seat next to me, and noticed a gold "Jesus First" pin on the lapel of my coat.

"Oh, you must be one of those members of Thomas Road Baptist Church where Jerry Falwell is pastor."

I noted his pejorative "one of those members," so I knew he must either dislike our brand of Christianity or tolerate evangelical Christians. He asked, "Why do you wear that 'Jesus First' pin?"

"Because I'm proud to be a Christian," I responded with a smile. Then added, "I want everyone to know I belong to Jesus Christ and He is 'First' in my life."

"Why's that?" was his simple response. This was a perfect open door.

So I told him that I had become a Christian at age 17 and God

called me into the ministry. I explained I had been to college and
seminary and that I was involved in training ministers and missionaries.

"I think I know what a missionary is," he explained. But then
he asked, "But what do your missionaries do?"

That was an open door to share the heart of Christianity. I
explained how young men and women were sent to people over-
seas to preach the gospel and start New Testament churches. At
Liberty University we encourage students after graduation to go to
foreign countries, share the message of Jesus, win people to Christ,
and in essence influence their cultures with the gospel.

"Why do that?" He talked of wasting their lives living among
people who were are the most part happy with their religion.
"What's wrong with being a Buddhist or a Hindu?" Then he added
a comment that if we could get Muslims to become Christians,
they would not blow up themselves and others.

"But they are lost without Christ," I said, jumping ahead of
what he was thinking. I tried to explain that people without Christ
would go to the grave "lost." This was a phrase he did not understand. When I used the word "hell," he reacted negatively.

"You Baptists put everyone in hell that doesn't agree with you!"

"No," I countered. "It's not a Baptist belief; all Christians
believe in hell and all Christians believe those outside Jesus Christ
are judged by God."

The man answered, "I find it difficult to believe a so-called
loving God would throw someone into hell just because he did not
believe in Jesus."

The problem was that the man had a wrong view of a person's standing before God; he did not believe in the sinfulness of

mankind that condemns all people. Also he had a wrong view of God, believing that He is only loving and forgiving. He did not know about the holiness and justice of God, that He must judge each offense against Him.

The Heathen Are Lost and Going to Hell

Point

The Bible teaches that there is no salvation apart from Jesus Christ. Those who have never accepted Jesus Christ are lost and are condemned to hell. Those who have never heard the gospel have an inborn knowledge of God, and yet they have rejected that knowledge of God (Rom 1:18–19). Also the Bible teaches that their conscience witnesses to them of "rightness" and "wrongness," but they have chosen to do what is wrong. The Bible teaches that sin is a universal condition of all people (3:23) that has separated them from God (Isa 59:2) and leads to death (Rom 6:23). Jesus died for the world (John 3:16), and only those who believe in Him will enjoy eternal life with the Father in heaven (John 14:16; Acts 4:12).

Counterpoint

"Universalists" believe all people will eventually go to heaven. They believe those who have never heard of Jesus Christ but are sincere in their beliefs and worship of God will be judged by a different standard, and because of their sincerity, they can make it to heaven. They maintain that because God is fair and loving, He would not send a person to hell without an opportunity for salvation. Universalists tend to deny the severity of God's judgment; some even deny hell. They believe those who have never heard the gospel will be judged in a different way from those who have heard of Jesus. Also some universalists believe God will give people after death another chance to gain salvation.

The businessman's contention that the heathen are not really lost was not the first time I had heard that argument. At the end of my first year in college I was living at home and each night we had devotions around the family dining room table. My sister Martha was entering her second year of high school when she announced God was calling her to become a missionary to Japan.

My mother might have been saved at the time, but probably not. My mother was perfectly willing for me to go into full-time Christian work, but she objected to Martha going to a foreign mission field.

"You don't want to do that," my mother argued directly with Martha. She told her, "The Japanese don't need you; almost the entire nation is Shintoist, and they are very religious."

Martha answered, "They won't go to heaven without Jesus."

But mother was convinced they did not need Christianity. She told Martha, "If a Shinto woman carries rice to her Shinto god shelf and prays sincerely, she will go to heaven when she dies." Mother explained that sincerity, sacrifice, and prayer would get them to heaven.

"No, Mother," Martha answered, "they are lost in sin."

The discussion went back and forth for about 10 minutes. Then I interrupted and quoted John 14:6, "Jesus told him, 'I am the way, the truth, and the life. No one comes to the Father except through Me." I emphasized the last part of the verse: "no one comes to the Father except though Me."

Mother finally stopped the discussion, "Well, if that's the way it is, I must be lost too because I believe sincerity is enough, the same way that Shinto woman believes."

I did not know how to answer her; she was my own mother and I did not want simply to just win an argument. I closed my Bible and went to bed.

But God was at work. Two weeks later my mother gave a testimony at our church's prayer meeting. "I'm thrilled Martha's going as a missionary to Japan. They are lost without Christ; they can be saved only by Jesus." Then my mother showed a deep smile that told me she was probably saved. She announced, "And for the first time I realize I'm saved and know it."

Why Universalists Think Some Heathens Who Have Not Heard the Gospel Will Go to Heaven

Counterpoint

- Some universalists believe the Bible teaches that everyone can be saved.
- Some universalists believe God will give them heathen a second chance after death.
- Some universalists believe God wants everyone to be saved because He is a good and loving God. Therefore He will work out some plan for them to enter heaven, even if they have never heard the gospel or the name Jesus Christ.
- Some universalists believe God will use a different standard to judge the heathen.

1. *Some universalists believe the Bible teaches that everyone can be saved.* (The word *universalists* is used here to include those who believe all worshippers of any god or religion will gain heaven based on their sincerity). Other universalists believe there is a plan for all to go to heaven, apart from their religion or belief.

Some universalists teach that all tribes will be recognized in heaven. They quote Rev 5:9 and 7:9, "They sang a new song . . . from every nation, tribe, people, and language" (Rev. 5:9; 7:9). They say the word "every" suggests the inclusive nature of salvation.

Yes, the Bible says that some will be saved out of every tribe and language group; but it does not say that *all* people from every tribe and language will be save. Also, it does not say that people from every generation of every tribe will be saved. In fact the Bible says, "This good news . . . will be proclaimed in all the world . . . and then the end will come" (Matt 24:14). When every tribe is reached with the gospel, and some are converted from every tribe, then Jesus may return.

Again, some universalists believe that many will be saved from all parts of the earth based on Matt 8:11. "Many will come from east and west and recline at the table . . . in the kingdom of heaven." They say phrase "east and west" is a description of the entire world, and so they believe the entire world will be represented in heaven.

But they fail to note the word "many" in this verse. Does God tell us how many? Did not Jesus say of salvation that "few find it" (Matt 7:14)? Obviously the word "many" and "few" are relative words without an exact number. Some will be saved from the entire earth because of missionary activity, not from any other means.

Other universalists refer to Matt 24:31, "His elect from the four winds, from one end of the sky to the other." The phrase "four winds" represents the whole earth; therefore they claim that people from all nations of the earth will be saved.

Karl Barth, a neo-orthodox theologian in the last century, held what is called "biblical universalism." As a universalist he wrote, "We have no theological right to set any sort of limits to the lovingkindness of God."[1] But Cornelius Van Til, a strong Presbyterian apologist, wrote about Barth's opinion, "For Barth, man, as sinner, is, to be sure, under the wrath of God, but this wrath is, itself, a form of the all-overreaching grace of God. There is no eternal punishment for those who are in Christ [because] there are no men who are not in Christ."[2]

2. *Some universalists believe God will give the heathen a second chance after death.* They believe that God will give them a chance after death, or He will deal with them differently in judgment, or He will embrace them in His love and mercy and take them to heaven. However, the Bible teaches the need to make a decision in this life (John 8:24; Heb 3:7–8), because punishment of the unsaved follows immediately after death, "It is appointed for people to die once–and after this, judgment" (Heb 9:27). The Bible also teaches that after death people go immediately to heaven or hell. Paul wrote that when a Christian dies, he is "out of the body and at home with the Lord" (2 Cor 5:8). The unsaved go immediately to hell. The rich man who was unrighteous in this life "died, and was buried; and in being in torment in Hades, he looked up" (Luke 16:22–23).

Norman Geisler asks the question, "Is there a second chance?" He answers this way:

> Many cults believe that God will give a second chance after death to those who never heard the Gospel. Orthodox Christians reject this. The Bible declares that "Just as man is destined to die once, and after that to face judgment" (Heb. 9:27). The urgency with which Scripture speaks of making one's decision now in this life (Prov. 29:1; John 8:24; Heb. 3:7–13; 2 Pet. 3:9) is strong evidence that there is no second chance. The fact that people immediately go to either heaven or hell (Luke 16:19–31; 2 Cor. 5:8; Rev. 19:20) indicates that a decision must be made in this life.[3]

But the issue is not whether the heathen have heard the gospel or whether they are ignorant of God's requirements; the issue is that people are lost because they have sinned against Him (Rom 3:23).

3. *Some universalists believe God wants everyone to be saved because He is a good and loving God.* They argue, "Does not God want everyone saved?" They note that God "wants everyone to be saved" (1 Tim 2:4). They also contend that since "the LORD is good to everyone" (Ps 145:9), He will save everyone. They may even point to Jesus' words in John 10:16, "I have other sheep that are not of this fold." They teach that God will take to heaven sheep in the Islamic fold, the Hindu fold, the Buddist fold, and the animist fold.

Virgil Warren wrote that he could not help wondering about the justice as well as the compassion of a God who assigns to eternal torment people who, for reasons beyond their control, never heard about fellowship with him through Jesus Christ. . . . Our opinion is that scripture does not automatically assign the unevangelized to endless hell.[4]

But the fact that God loves everyone does not mean everyone will be saved. God expressed His love to all, in that Jesus died for all (1 John 2:2), but that does not guarantee salvation for everyone. God has called on everyone to repent. "God now commands all people everywhere to repent" (Acts 17:30).

4. *Some universalists believe God will use a different standard to judge the heathen.* Many non-Christian's believe that those who have never heard of Jesus Christ will be judged differently from those who have heard the gospel. But that would make God inconsistent. How would God judge differently those who have heard and those who have not heard? The Bible calls God true (Deut 32:4); and (Pss 25:10; 86:11 characterized by truths). And Jesus

called Himself truth (John 14:6). Truth is defined as "an established or verified fact, principle."[5] Also truth is what is consistent with itself. Then how can God be consistent and treat one group of people differently from the way He treats another group?

If some people end up in heaven by being good or by some arbitrary decision by God, then "Christ died for nothing" (Gal 2:21). And if Jesus died needlessly, who could ever trust a God like that?

No, Jesus died to give everyone an opportunity to go to heaven. God offers heaven to all who will believe in Jesus and accept His solution for them. God's justice and love are seen together in God. As Geisler writes, "God's justice demands that he condemns all sinners, but his love compels him to provide salvation for all who by his grace will believe. For "Everyone who calls on the name of the Lord will be saved" (Rom 10:13)."[6]

Point

- The heathen are lost because Jesus is the only way to heaven.
- The heathen are lost because they are sinners.
- The heathen are lost because they have an inborn knowledge of God in their hearts but have rejected Him.
- The heathen are lost because they have not obeyed their conscience.

1. *The heathen are lost because Jesus is the only way to heaven.* No normal, loving human being wants to see another person punished and relegated to hell. But Christians believe that the heathen are lost because Jesus excludes all who have not believed in Him. Jesus said, "I am the way, the truth, and the life. No one comes to the Father except through Me" (John 14:6). This is a declaration by

Jesus, not the desire of any human. (See chapter 5, "Is Jesus the Only Way?")

When Peter preached to those who rejected Jesus Christ, he reminded them, "There is salvation in no one else, for there is no other name under heaven given to people by which we must be saved" (Acts 4:12). Notice two exclusive statements! The first negative is, "There is salvation in no one else." Peter excluded all other ways to heaven, except by Jesus Christ. His second negative excludes any person going to heaven except through Jesus, "no other name . . . by which we must be saved." This double negative says only those who believe in Jesus Christ will go to heaven, and it excludes all other ways to heaven.

Jesus said "many" will not be in heaven because they will not come in at the narrow gate and He said only a "few" find heaven. "Enter through the narrow gate. For the gate is wide and the road is broad that leads to destruction, and there are many who go through it. How narrow is the gate and difficult the road that leads to life, and few find it" (Matt 7:13–14).

2. *The heathen are lost because they are sinners.* The indictment in the Bible is that all have sinned. All are sinners by birth as evidenced by David's confession, "I was sinful when my mother conceived me" (Ps 51:5). Sin came originally from our first parents Adam and Eve and was charged (imputed) to the account of each person, "Death spread to all men, because all sinned" (Rom 5:12).

What is the result? None are righteous, we "are all under sin . . . there is no one righteous, not even one" (Rom 3:9–10). Then because everyone has a sin nature received at birth, they sin; thereby reflecting the universality of sin. "All have sinned and fall short of the glory of God" (3:23).

What are the consequences of sin? "The wages of sin is death" (Rom 6:23). People are not lost and go to hell because they have

---

The Law of God

God has laws by which He relates to mankind and by which He manages the universe. God created man and woman in His own image to glorify Himself and to worship and do His will. The first couple disobeyed God's law and deserved to be punished eternally from His presence. God could not truthfully and arbitrarily forgive, nor could He allow punishment to be set aside. God's law demands punishment for any disobedience of His laws. God sent His Son to live under the law and perfectly keep the law. Then God allowed His Son to be punished in the place of humans. Jesus' death represented an eternal separation from the Father. And the blood of Jesus which represented His death was offered to cleanse sinners and make them presentable to God. All who will accept Jesus Christ and His death will be forgiven and will be taken to heaven at their death.

---

not heard the gospel; they are lost because they are sinners. "People are lost not because they are ignorant of God's law, but because they have sinned against Him."[7]

If a person is given a traffic ticket for speeding in a school zone, the offender cannot plead innocence simply because he did not see the speed-limit sign. The issue is his speeding, not his ignorance of the law. So with the unsaved. The issue is not whether they have heard the gospel, the issue is the fact of their sin.

3. *The heathen are lost because they have an inborn knowledge of God in their hearts but have rejected Him.* God has revealed Himself to all people; as a result they are without excuse. All are born with an awareness of God. Because people know God but reject Him,

they are "without excuse" (Rom 1:20). "For God's wrath is revealed from heaven against all godlessness and unrighteousness of people who by their unrighteousness suppress the truth, since what can be known about God is evident among them" (1:18–19).

And what do the heathen know about God? "From the creation of the world His invisible attributes, that is, His eternal power and divine nature, have been clearly seen, being understood through what He has made" (Rom 1:20). As a result of what they know about God, they "are without excuse" (v. 20).

The heathen know there is a God, but they reject Him. However, they devise their own way to heaven, though, idols and false religious practices. But an idol is not God, and man's ways are not acceptable to Him; God punishes the heathen because through they know Him they reject Him. They have rejected what they have known in their hearts.

Three times Paul said, "God delivered them over" (Rom 1:24, 26,28). When God gave them up, He also gave them over to sinfulness, uncleanliness, and all forms of filthiness and rebellion against God. "He delivered them over to a worthless mind to do what is morally wrong" (v. 28).

Norman Geisler asks, "Is it fair to condemn those who have not heard?" And he answers,

> Yes. . . . First, through general revelation they know about his "eternal power and divine nature" (Rom. 1:20). They are aware that he "made heaven and earth and sea and everything in them" (Acts 14:15). They are aware that God "has not left himself without testimony: He has shown kindness by giving you rain from heaven and crops in their seasons" (Acts 14:17).[8]

Yes, the heathen have knowledge of God and seek Him by idols, false religious views, religious exercises, and they are even afraid of black magic and demonism. "Though they knew God, they did not glorify Him as God" (Rom 1:21).

"God delivered them over" to a life of all kinds of sin and false religious practices, because they rejected Him. If they had recognized God in their hearts and had believed in Him, He would have sent someone to preach the gospel to them and offer them salvation.

So because the heathen know God but have rejected Him, God has no obligation to do anything more for them. "Even though God has revealed himself to the heathen in creation and in conscience, fallen humanity has universally rejected that light. Hence, God is not obligated to give them any more light, since they have turned from the light they have."[9]

But that does not mean that God did not do something. In mercy and love God sends His missionaries to preach the gospel to them. God encourages His intercessor to pray for them. God sends missionaries to win individuals to Jesus Christ, baptize them into a local church, and teach them the ways of God (Matt 28:19–20). All this is because God is "not wanting any to perish" (2 Pet 3:9).

If any unbeliever truly sought God through the general revelation, God would provide the special revelation sufficient for salvation. After God led Peter to the Gentile Cornelius, Peter declared: "I now realize how true it is that God does not show favoritism but accepts men from every nation who fear him and do what is right" (Acts 10:34–35 NIV). The writer of Hebrews tells us that those who seek, find. "He rewards those who earnestly seek him" (Heb 11:6).[10]

Missionaries who work among the heathen know certain things about their knowledge of God. First, all heathen know there is a God, and they all have different names for God.

Second, there are no philosophical atheists among the heathen who want to argue against the existence of God, nor are there pragmatic atheists who reject His existence because of some problems in their lives. No, the heathen know there is a God, but they will not accept Him.

Third, the heathen have developed false worship systems and substitute gods for the real God. They have a widespread sense of dread and frightfulness, and they take part in all kinds of religious activities to placate their concept of God.

Fourth, the heathen know they have sinned. They are not righteous, nor do they think heaven is owed to them, or that God will somehow accept them because of their own righteousness.

Fifth, they seem afraid of God's punishment, and they seem to walk in dread of what will happen to them because of their sin.

4. *The heathen are lost because they have not obeyed their conscience.* Every person is born with a conscience, that is, an inborn sense of right or wrong that comes from an inward awareness of God. The heathen have not obeyed their God-given conscience.

"God will punish the Gentiles when they sin. . . . When Gentiles, who do not have God's written law, instinctively follow what the laws says, they show that in their hearts (Rom 2:12,14 NLT), they know right from wrong.

Those who argue in favor of salvation for the heathen apart from the gospel are perhaps playing mental games. Possibly this is because they are trying to excuse their own sin before God. Or perhaps they are trying to justify their own lifestyle or their disobedience to the Word of God. They want God to give them a second chance after death, or they want God to be merciful in judging them, or they are hoping by some chance that they might merit salvation. So they identify with the heathen when they argue for heathen salvation, and hence are arguing for their own salvation.

However, in reverse the born-again Christian knows he has eternal life because he has accepted Jesus Christ as his Savior. When someone turns to Jesus Christ, he realizes that salvation is a narrow door, and that door is Jesus. When he walks through that narrow door, he enters on the "straight path" that leads to eternal life. Those who accept Jesus Christ fully embrace Him for salvation, knowing there is no other salvation, there is no other way to heaven, there is no other means of salvation (Acts 4:12). In accepting Jesus' narrow way, they show that those who have not entered the narrow gate are lost and will go to hell.

Six-Question Wrap-up

1. Are the heathen really lost? Absolutely! Every page of the Bible reveals the sinfulness of man, and as a result of sin people are lost and are condemned to hell.
2. Will God set anyone free on a technicality, such as courts might do? No! Everyone knows he is a sinner, and everyone is born with the knowledge of God in his heart. So everyone who has not acknowledged God, nor sought God, nor received Christ as his Savior will be condemned.
3. Is God fair to condemn the heathen who have not heard the gospel? God is always fair, He cannot be otherwise. Everyone is commanded to repent and turn to God. Everyone has had a chance to turn to God.

4. How will God respond when a heathen honestly seeks salvation? The Bible gives illustrations of God sending a human instrument to preach the gospel to honest seekers. For example Philip was sent to the Ethiopian eunuch, and Peter was sent to preach to Cornelius. All who honestly seek God and heaven will have a gospel messenger sent to them.

5. What is the responsibility of Christians? They are told to "go into all the world and preach the gospel to the whole creation" (Mark 16:15). This means going to every person and preaching the message of the gospel to them. Once they believe in Christ, they are to be baptized. "Go, therefore, and make disciples of all nations, baptizing them in the name of the Father and of the Son and of the Holy Spirit" (Matt 28:19). And believers are to seek to bring new Christians to maturity, "teaching them to observe everything I have commanded you" (v. 20).

6. How is this responsibility carried out? Believers should support their church that sends missionaries to preach the gospel in heathen tribes (Acts 13:1–3). They should give finances to missionaries preaching the gospel to those who have never heard (Phil 4:14–17). They should pray for the heathen to be saved. And when God calls someone to go, he must obey and do as God commands (John 15:16).

Wrap-up

Some have argued that Christians are guilty of bigotry because they think only their view is right. They say it is "narrow-minded" to limit heaven to those who come through Jesus Christ. But truth is narrow. Is it bigotry to say people cannot survive without food or water? No, it is truthful to say people need food and water to live.

Is it bigotry to say no one can hang-glide to the moon? No. Only truthful; it's life-saving. Only a space rocket can fly to the moon, no matter how much a person may want to hang-glide to there. Similarly only Jesus is the way to heaven. He said, "You will know the truth, and the truth will set you free" (John 8:32).

Sincerity is not enough, not matter what religion a person follows. Sincerity will not substitute for the truth. Sincerity does not get a young man to the National Football League, nor does sincerity win "Miss America" for a young lady. There are rules to follow, laws to obey, and a proper path that leads to every desired goal in life. So God has rules, laws, and a path that leads to eternal life. "There is a way that seems right to a man, but its end is the way to death" (Prov 14:12). Therefore when a person knows Jesus is the "the way, the truth, and the life . . . to the Father" (John 14:6), he must come by way of Him.

DISCUSSION QUESTIONS

1. What are the chances of anyone getting to heaven by sincerity or religious practices?
2. Are not almost all other religions intolerant? Do not they claim they are the only way to life after physical death? Then why do "universalists" not attack them as they attack Christianity?
3. Why do so many non-Christians attack Christianity for its alleged intolerance?
4. What are some ways of convincing an honest seeker that the heathen are lost and that they must be reached with the gospel?

5. What is the strongest argument given by universalists for their position, and how can it be answered?

6. Because the heathen are lost, what should each Christian begin doing to reach them?

Endnotes

1. J. Estabrook and B. Thompson, *Apologetics Press: Reason and Revelation,* 21 (June 2001): 41-46, http://www.apologeticspress.org/articles/469 (accessed August 2, 2010).

2. Ibid.

3. N. L. Geisler, "'Heathen,' Salvation of," in *Baker Encyclopedia of Christian Apologetics* (Grand Rapids: Baker, 1999307, http://www.ankerberg.org/Articles/Salvation/Salvation%20PDF/salvation-heathen.pdf, (accessed August 2, 2010).

4. V. Warren, *What the Bible Says about Salvation* (Joplin, 140: College Press, 1982) 104–5 (emphasis his), http://222.apologeticspress.ort/articles/469.

5. *Webster's New World Dictionary,* s.v. "truth."

6. Geisler, "'Heathen,' Salvation of," 306.

7. Estabrook and Thompson, *Apologetics Press: Reason & Revelation* (accessed July 29, 2010).

8. Geisler, "'Heathen,' Salvation of," 306.

9. Ibid.

10. Ibid.

Chapter 8

Is Hell a Real Place That Lasts for Eternity?

by Alex McFarland

People sometimes portray hell as a party zone. "When I die," more than one person has said, "I want to go to hell, 'cause that's where all my friends will be!" But if he knew what Scripture says about hell, he would think twice about that. Hell is a place of eternal separation from God, a place of great suffering and the ultimate judgment on a life spent in rebellion to God.

This chapter could be titled, "Divine Retribution: Reconciling the Goodness of God with the Reality of Hell." Twenty-first-century people (even some evangelical Christians) often shy away from acknowledging the reality of hell. Yet it is often mentioned in the Bible. And Jesus often spoke about hell. Hell is real, and Christians are remiss if they do not recognize that.

Hell is a source of much doctrinal controversy. Western culture has in a sense done away with hell. It is a scary concept and it is difficult to think that a loving God would do something as awful as send someone to a place as terrible as hell. Therefore many people cover up the idea of hell and seek to make it less of a bad place, or they say there is no such place. Others say hell is just a place of purification where a person is cleansed and then released to heaven.

"But I will show you the One to fear: Fear Him who has authority to throw people into hell after death. Yes, I say to you, this is the One to fear!" (Luke 12:5).

One time a TV talk-show host said, "God is love, and the God I believe in would never send someone to hell!" The audience applauded enthusiastically as she passionately stated her position about the afterlife. A panel of guests had been assembled to explain various views about death, heaven, hell, and God's judgment. Of those authors and scholars, only one individual, an evangelical minister defended the biblical teaching about hell. And as the program progressed, both audience and interviewer seemed increasingly hostile to that lone evangelical panelist.

Surveys show that in the West belief in a literal hell is at an all-time low, and its most vocal opponents include some clergy. Not long ago a survey of born-again Christians by the Barna Research Group concluded that Christians are often ignorant about the biblical doctrine of hell. Even though 98 percent of those surveyed said their Christian faith is very important in their life, some of the survey's findings were discouraging. For example:

- Thirty-eight percent believe that if a person is generally good, he can earn a place in heaven. (This contradicts the Bible, which says eternal life is "the gift of God"; see Rom 6:23; Eph 2:8–9.)

- Fifty percent said that Satan is "not a living being but is a symbol of evil." (The Bible clearly identifies Satan as a living being, calling him "your adversary"; see 1 Pet 5:8.)
- Thirty-one percent of born-again Christians agree with the statement, "while He lived on earth, Jesus committed sins, like other people."[1] (The Bible says that Jesus was perfect; He never sinned; see Heb 4:14–15.)

In a world of psychic hotlines, horoscopes, Wicca, and alternative spirituality, Christians must be able to share their beliefs effectively. They must proclaim clearly, consistently, gently, and lovingly, the possibility of heaven and the warnings of hell.

Apologist Peter Kreeft addressed the fact that ignorance or denial of the biblical teachings about hell comes often from within the church. "Of all the doctrines of Christianity, hell is probably the most difficult to defend, the most burdensome to believe, and the first to be abandoned."[2]

For example F. W. Farrar, chaplain to Queen Victoria, labeled the doctrine of hell as "blasphemy against the merciful God." He and many others from the Victorian period wanted to change people's views of hell. They did not like to think about hell as a real place because of how awful it is. "Whereas preachers from earlier eras were concerned to save persons from punishment in hell, Farrar and his like-minded colleagues were determined to save their congregations from the fear of hell."[3]

However, this is not a topic to be ignored. Hell is a real place where those who do not turn to Christ as their Savior and Lord will be allowed to go, where they will be separated forever from God. The task of believers is to tell people the truth, even when it is not pleasant. Although hell may be offensive to talk about, it is reality and a fact that cannot be avoided.

Jonathan Edwards was a fiery preacher who played a key role in America's First Great Awakening, a spiritual revival that swept the country in the mid-1700s. In what is perhaps his most famous sermon, "Sinners in the Hands of an Angry God," Edwards said:

> So that, whatever some have imagined and pretended about promises made to natural men's earnest seeking and knocking, it is plain and manifest, that whatever pains a natural man takes in religion, whatever prayers he makes, till he believes in Christ, God is under no manner of obligation to keep him a moment from eternal destruction.
>
> So that, thus it is that natural men are held in the hand of God, over the pit of hell; they have deserved the fiery pit, and are already sentenced to it; and God is dreadfully provoked, his anger is as great towards them as to those that are actually suffering the executions of the fierceness of his wrath in hell, and they have done nothing in the least to appease or abate that anger, neither is God in the least bound by any promise to hold them up one moment; the devil is waiting for them, hell is gaping for them, the flames gather and flash about them, and would fain lay hold on them, and swallow them up; the fire bent up in their own hearts is struggling to break out: and they have no interest in any Mediator, there are no means within reach that can be any security to them. In short, they have no refuge, nothing to take hold of; all that preserves them every moment is the mere arbitrary will, and uncovenanted, unobliged forbearance of an incensed God.[4]

Points

- Hell is a teaching essential to Christian doctrine. Scripture paints a picture of what hell is like, and more importantly, that it is real.
- Take away hell, and you wind up with humans who have no free will. We would not have a choice about the afterlife. Heaven would be our only option.
- There is no contradiction between a loving God and the reality of hell. The Bible presents both. Though seemingly incompatible, the goodness of God and the reality of hell can be reconciled.
- God does not actually send people to hell. People choose to abandon God and He allows it. God does not force people to worship Him, or to experience the joy of His presence.

Counterpoints

- Hell is not a real place. It's just a made up thing that Christians use to scare people into converting.
- Hell may be real, but not the way the Bible paints it. After death, lost souls are eventually annihilated. They won't suffer eternally. Rather than suffer for evil, people are just destroyed, or somehow disappear.
- No human with a conscience would ever accept the idea that people will suffer eternally in a place as horrific as hell. A truly loving God would never allow such a thing.

Objections to Hell

The main objection nonbelievers have against hell is that it simply does not exist. Believers hold several views.

Some believe in annihilationism. They believe hell is real and that those who go there do not come back, but they believe that at death people are annihilated. They cease to exist.

Those who hold this view misinterpret Matt 5:22. The word used for hell here is *Gehenna*, which comes from Greek geenna, a Greek form of the Hebrew words *ge hinnom* ("Valley of Hinnom"). This valley ran outside the walls of Jerusalem and was used in Old Testament times for human sacrifices to the pagan god Molech. King Josiah put a stop to this dreadful practice (2 Kgs 23:10), and the Valley of Hinnom came to be used as a place where human excrement and rubbish were disposed of and burned. It was, in effect, a giant trash dump. The fire of Gehenna never went out, and the worms never died, so it came to be used symbolically of the place of divine punishment.

Annihilationists focus on the idea that what goes there is burned up. Edward W. Fudge, one of the main proponents of this view, holds that this idea means the fires destroy completely. But he "appears to underinterpret *Gehenna*. He does this in part by committing the exegetical fallacy of confusing referent (the Valley of Hinnom outside of Jerusalem and the mundane burning that allegedly occurred there) and sense (a place of extraordinary punishment prepared by God for his enemies). . . . the latter [is what] Jesus warns against; the connotative meaning (sense) of Matt 5:22 is primarily God's hell, not a Judean waste disposal site."[5] In short, Jesus used the idea of *Gehenna* as an image so His audience could sense the reality of hell.

Annihilationists also cite Matt 5:29–30. They consider the whole body going to hell to mean a complete loss of one's person or identity. They view it as a complete destruction of a person's body and soul. But being thrown into hell is "active punishment, not a 'passive loss.'"[6]

Some annihilationists also cite Mark 9:47–48. Fudge specifically states that the worm and unquenchable fire will destroy until nothing remains. This is illogical, though, because a fire that destroys until nothing is left is quenched. If everything is burned, there would be no more fire. And "destruction cannot be both 'completed' and therefore over with and at the same time 'last for eternity.'"[7]

So David Edwards and John Stott state, "Souls seem to be intrinsically immortal, immortal by their essence, so that it would be as self-contradictory to have a soul cease to exist as to have a circle become a square."[8]

Others object to the biblical view of hell by saying that hell would be in contradiction to God's victory over evil. However, people who hold this view often use 1 Cor 15:24–28 to make their point. But Rev 20:10 gives the answer, for Satan will be in hell forever. Satan, the prince of evil, will be held in this judgment for all eternity. Revelation 21 and 22 make clear that heaven is a place uncontaminated by evil. Hell, as well as heaven, will continue forever. But their coexistence does not contradict Scripture or God's sovereignty and power. Hell reveals God's justice and love. He will use hell to bring about lasting justice.

Another belief that denies the reality of hell is called universalism, the belief that everyone will eventually be saved. Universalists believe no matter how bad a person has been, he will eventually be united with God in heaven. There are several different forms of universalism. A fairly prominent Christian version says that hell is simply a way station for purification where those who do not come to faith on earth will be purified in hell and then released to heaven. Then there are others who think that there is no such place as hell, because God could not send people to such a terrible place.

Most universalists agree that the Bible gives no warrant for this belief, but they continue to be universalists out of a desire that no one should go to hell. But their love is not a pure form of love, for it lacks justice. The fact that a person does not want to accept something does not make it untrue. Universalism is very popular, though, because it is "politically correct." It is viewed as "nice," for it does not hurt anyone's feelings. And it is supposedly tolerant. Universalism allows people to get away with doing as they please and not having to face the consequences. These people are not living in reality! Hell is reality, and if they do not face that fact they are either themselves on their way to hell or allowing others to go there because they do not want to seem to be "forcing religion" down someone's throat.

Universalists do not hold to a proper view of salvation, because if everyone can be saved, then what was the point of Jesus dying on the cross?

Others object to the notion of eternal conscious torment. Theologian John Stott wrote, "The concept of eternal conscious torment [is] intolerable. [I] do not understand how people can live with it without cauterizing their feelings or cracking under the strain."[9] Jesus, however, did not find the idea of everlasting punishment intolerable. Instead He seemed to have it on His mind constantly but He did not "crack under the strain." There is another sort of "cauterizing" that Stott seems not to have noted, one that has affected society in tangible ways, namely, moral relativism. Getting rid of everlasting justice leads to today's idea of tolerance and acceptance. Robert W. Yarbrough writes, "If one kind of hell is found in the Bible's story of a loving but zealous God who consigns the wicked, whom he deems deserving, to permanent woe, a plausible analogy might be the vacuous moral vertigo in which much contemporary human consciousness languishes."[10]

This leads to another objection, which views hell as the greatest of all evils. How could God, who is all loving, send people to a place like hell? The answer is ultimately in the juxtaposition of justice and love seen most clearly at the cross. How can God be both loving and forgiving and yet just and punish sin? The answer is Jesus. He sent his Son to pay the price of sin so that justice would be served and people can receive forgiveness.

To be just, God must punish sin; He cannot let evil reign (Rom 6:23). Those who sin must pay the price, which is death. Death here is referring to hell. This is not just a physical death; it is a spiritual death. Those who do not choose Christ are separated from Him for all eternity. But His love is also seen in that He does not annihilate those who do not choose Him, for that would go against His nature. He cannot destroy the soul, which is good. But He can banish what is evil. He allows the one who does not choose Him to have what he or she wanted, that is, separation from Him forever. They did not desire His presence, and so He allows them to be forever removed from Him.

As Steven Ladd wrote, "If all evils were removed from the universe we would not know the good, for the good is better known by comparison with evil, as health is most appreciated by those who have lost it."[11]

And Kreeft and Tacelli reason this way:

> If there is no reason for believing in the detested doctrine of hell, there is also no reason to believe in the most beloved doctrine in Christianity: that God is love. The beloved doctrine is the reason critics most frequently give for disbelieving the detested doctrine; yet the two stand on exactly the same foundation.[12]

If a person denies hell because he finds the notion unbearable and undesirable, then why not drop other parts of Christianity that are supposedly unbearable or undesirable? The reality of hell is inextricably tied to the person and work of Christ. If there is no hell, then one's understanding of who Jesus is and what He did must be thoroughly revised. "In other words, removing hell is not like removing one stone from a pile and leaving all the others untouched. It is like removing a vital organ from a body; all the others are affected and eventually killed."[13]

The Reality of Hell

Doubting hell because a person finds it difficult to believe would mean people can change whatever they want because they dislike it, which is the first step down toward relativism.

God created mankind for the best of all worlds. He has given people the ability to have free choice. They can decide what to do; He does not *make* them do what is right. People have a choice. And an understanding of free will leads one to view hell as an essential Christian doctrine.

God will triumph over evil when it is the perfect time. As Jesus said, "I have told you these things so that in Me you may have peace. You will have suffering in this world. Be courageous! I have conquered the world" (John 16:33). Love is the greatest good (Matt 22:36–37), but love is impossible without free choice. One does not truly love someone if that person forces him to love him. That is not love. God wants people to know the greatest kind of love through free choice. He gave this to mankind even though He knew people would choose to do the opposite of good and bring evil into the world. Instead of destroying humanity to get rid of evil, God decided to give people the greatest choice and the greatest good of all.

This is referred to as the "crucial" answer to the problem of evil, because it is the crux of the matter. The English term *crucial* derives from the Latin crux, which means "cross." In the end the cross of Christ serves as the ultimate divine answer to the problem of evil. Mankind took the life of the innocent Son of God (Acts 2:23). At the same time the crucifixion of Jesus Christ is God's ultimate act of benevolence and power. There the Father gave up his Son (John 3:16; 2 Cor 5:21). And the righteous Son, in the perfect expression of genuine human freedom (Mark 10:45), gave up His life (Rom 5:8; 2 Cor 5:21) so that people can be reconciled to God. Evil is indeed present in God's world, but it will not prevail.[14]

God has given us the answer to the problem of evil. It was not a problem until mankind brought it into the world through a choice to do what was not good. The true problem for most people who struggle with the problem of evil is a heart issue, perhaps because of the pride of not wanting to admit they are at fault. All one need do for the answer is to look at the cross and remember God has already provided the greatest good and if a person accepts that, then one day he will be in paradise with Him and evil will be defeated.

At one and the same time Jesus' crucifixion filled God's plan and was the greatest crime ever perpetrated! The tension between God's sovereignty and human freedom displayed in the cross is indeed mysterious. To tamper with either aspect produces terrible results. To deny human responsibility transforms the perpetrators into God's servants who do good when they crucify the Son of God. To minimize divine sovereignty transforms the cross into an emergency measure of God. Such transformations are wrong in the extreme. Inscrutably the cross is both God's will, without tarnishing him with evil, and the culpable deeds of evildoers, without making them puppets whose strings are pulled by God.[15]

Without hell, heaven becomes the default position. But heaven is not just a place of eternal bliss. It is the place where the redeemed will spend eternity worshipping God *in His presence.* Why, then, would anyone want to spend an eternity in the presence of God if he wanted nothing to do with Him during his temporal existence?

Heaven loses some of its attributes if hell does not exist. Without hell, one must get rid of free will. There is no choice if there is no hell. This also leads to moral relativism. If there is no hell, there is no difference between good and evil. If there is no hell, then Jesus also is not who He claims to be because people would not need a Savior. Faith is truly in vain if there is no hell. Christ's death was a mistake.

The Bible teaches that both heaven and hell are very real places and that each person will eventually spend eternity in one of these two places. Most of what is known about hell is straight from Jesus' mouth: "If your hand or your foot causes your downfall, cut it off and throw it away. It is better for you to enter life maimed or lame, than to have two hands or two feet and be thrown into the eternal fire. And if your eye causes your downfall, gouge it out and throw it away. It is better for you to enter life with one eye, rather than to have two eyes and be thrown into hellfire!" (Matt 18:8–9).

"And they will go away into eternal punishment, but the righteous into eternal life" (Matt 25:46).

"Do not be amazed at this, because a time is coming when all who are in the graves will hear His voice and come out—those who have done good things, to the resurrection of life, but those who have done wicked things, to the resurrection of judgment" (John 5:28–29).

Scripture's main description of hell is as a place of punishment (Matt 5:20–30; 24–25; Mark 9:42–48; Luke 16:19–31; 2 Thess 1:5–10; Heb 10:27–31; Jas 4:12; 5:1–5; 2 Pet 2:4–17; Jude 13–23;

and Rev 20:10–15). The punishment is just because it is deserved. Those in hell are in an inescapable, indescribable torment. It is also conscious punishment, and it is everlasting. A person cannot escape hell. Once there, he will always be there.

Another key emphasis in the Bible's descriptions of hell is that of destruction. This has led some to conclude that the Bible teaches annihilationism. But the idea of destruction in hell does not mean extinction. The words used refer to a thing that has lost its nature—it can never do what it was made to do. People were made to love God and worship Him, but because they decide to deny God forever, those in hell cannot fulfill their purpose any longer. That is what destruction in this sense means.

Banishment is the other key emphasis on hell. Those in hell are banished from heaven and from God. This is a final, everlasting separation described in Rev 22:14–15.

Implications If There Is No Hell

If a person believes there is no hell, then he must question all the other doctrines of the church and the inerrancy of Scripture. One cannot hold to Christianity and throw hell out the window. Also if hell is denied, Christ's authority is in question.

C. S. Lewis comments on the reality, characteristics, and rationality of hell.

> Some will not be redeemed. There is no doctrine which I would more willingly remove from Christianity than this, if it lay in my power. But is has the full support of Scripture and, specially, of our Lord's own words; it has always been held by Christendom, and it has the support of reason. . . .
>
> The characteristic of lost souls is "their rejection of

everything that is not simply themselves." . . . He has his last wish—to live wholly in the self and to make the best of what he finds there. And what he finds there is hell. . . .

In the long run, the answer to all those who object to the doctrine of hell is itself a question: "What are you asking God to do?" To wipe out all their past sins, and, at all costs, to give them a fresh start, smoothing every difficulty and offering every miraculous help? But He has done so, on Calvary.[16]

Interestingly Lewis points out that denial of hell's reality undermines Jesus' authority. Such denial also debases humans. How? To deny that man has free will counters the Christian concept that people are "image bearers" (Gen 1:26). Some humans exercise their will to reject God and His overtures. Lewis also said of hell, "The door of hell is locked on the inside."[17] "There are only two kinds of people in the end: those who say to God, 'Thy will be done,' and those to whom God says, in the end, '*Thy will be done.' All that are in hell, choose it.*"[18] In other words God allows people to choose not to be in His presence. By choosing to abandon God, people are choosing hell. This is an important point.

I would pay any price to be able to say truthfully "All will be saved." But my reason retorts, "Without their will, or with it?" If I say "Without their will," I at once perceive a contradiction; how can the supreme voluntary act of self-surrender be involuntary? If I say "With their will," my reason replies, "How if they will not give in?" . . .

The demand that God should forgive such a man while he remains what he is, is based on a confusion between condoning and forgiving. To condone an evil is simply to ignore it, to treat it as if it were good. But forgiveness needs to be accepted as well as offered if it is to be complete: and a man who admits no guilt can accept no forgiveness.[19]

The burden of acceptance of forgiveness remains with the sinner. One must accept the consequences of having free will, including his sins. Because of sin a person must accept Christ, who was the answer to sin. But those who do not do that must nonetheless accept the consequences of their sin. God would be unjust if He allowed them to escape the consequences of their actions, their desire to be free from Him.

People use their will to suppress what may be known of God. The Bible tells that God has shown Himself to people throughout history. The Bible further warns that people have willfully rejected the light they have been given. "For God's wrath is revealed from heaven against all godlessness and unrighteousness of people who by their unrighteousness suppress the truth" (Rom 1:18; 2:1–16). And Jesus said, "This, then, is the judgment: the light has come into the world, and people loved darkness rather than the light because their deeds were evil" (John 3:19).

Sin is present, hell is real, and humans choose them both in lieu of a revelatory, relational, redemptive, and restorative God. People are not free to reinvent, revise, or change biblical truths and Christian doctrines for mere accommodation. One must not evaluate truth based on what is popular, preferred, or politically correct. Truth must be evaluated based on God's Word.

Some opponents of the biblical view may not be trying to throw out the doctrine of hell; they may simply have trouble seeing how such a place can exist if God is love. But the answer is this: God lovingly offers forgiveness, but it must be accepted. It cannot be forced. Accepting the reality of hell does not make God vengeful or hateful. He is characterized by love and mercy, but also by justice and righteousness. Apologist J. P. Moreland says, "It's wrong to think God is simply a loving being, especially if you mean 'loving' in the sense that most Americans use that word today. Yes, God is a compassionate being, but he's also a just, moral, and pure being."[20]

The truth is that hell is necessary because God's holy and just nature demands that evil be punished. Similarly the cross was necessary because God's merciful nature demanded that salvation be offered.

Since everyone falls short of God's standard (Rom 3:23), they all deserve hell. Three points should be noted in this connection:

1. God is good (righteous, gracious, merciful).
2. Man is free (informed, volitional, fallen).
3. Therefore judgment is fair.

At the final judgment one thing will be patently clear: God is fair. And God is merciful and just. What is actually unfair is the fact that anyone will be in heaven. No one is good enough for heaven. The opportunity to enter God's holy presence illustrates His mercy and grace.

Jonathan Edwards reflected on the uncomfortable truth of hell: *"Tis dreadful, 'tis awful . . . but 'tis true."*[21] The Bible states that people loved darkness rather than light (John 3:19), and that Jesus is the only way to get to heaven (John 14:6; Rom 5:12–17). Recognition of what the Bible teaches about hell actually reveals a high view of Christ. In a way a denial of hell is reflective of a low Christology. The wisdom of Charles Spurgeon (1834–1892) comes from more than a century ago. "Think lightly of hell, and you will think lightly of the cross. Think little of the sufferings of lost souls, and you will soon think little of the Savior who delivers them."[22]

Those who fail to accept Christ's payment for their sins will go to hell. It is that simple. Heaven and hell are very real places. Whether a person will be in heaven or hell after death will depend on whether he chooses to accept God's gift and follow Jesus. About this most serious of subjects, it is the Christian's *privilege and duty to proclaim what God has clearly revealed. Hope is found in salvation through Christ alone!*

Bible Words That Describe
the Final State of the Lost

Sheol: An Old Testament word for the grave, or the place of the dead. It can mean the afterlife with either rewards or punishments (Gen 37:35; Job 33:24; and Ps 30:9). Those in Sheol are cut off from both God and man (2 Sam 12:23). God is present in Sheol (Job 26:6) but cannot be contacted (Ps 6:5). "Though the translation 'hell' can be misleading, there are references connecting Sheol with wickedness of life (Ps 9:17; Prov 5:5; . . . Ez. 32:23)."[23]

Gehenna: A word that in Hebrew means "Valley of Hinnom" (2 Kings 23:10). It is a symbolic name for hell, taken from a burning garbage dump near Jerusalem. The bodies of executed criminals were thrown into Gehenna (Matt 5:22,29–30; see also 10:28; 18:9; 23:15; 23:33; Mark 9:43–48; and Luke 12:5). Jesus often used the word *Gehenna* to describe hell (Mark 9:43–48). He also said that there would be "outer darkness" and "weeping and gnashing of teeth" there (Matt 8:12; 22:13).

Hell: The English translation of the words *sheol, gehenna,* and *hades.* It can mean the grave or the realm of the conscious dead. It is also referred to as a place of punishment, fire, brimstone, and eternal torment.

Hades: The unseen world, a place of torments. See Matt 11:23; 16:18; Luke 10:15; 16:23; Acts 2:27,31; Rev 1:18; 6:8; 20:13–14.

Tartarus: "For if God didn't spare the angels who sinned, but threw them down into Tartarus and delivered them to be kept in chains of darkness until judgment" (2 Pet 2:4). "Tartarus . . . is neither Sheol nor Hades nor hell, but the place where those angels whose special sin is referred to in that passage are confined, 'to be reserved unto judgment'; the region is described as 'pits of darkness.'"[24]

DISCUSSION QUESTIONS

1. Why do people want to hide from the reality of hell? How are some of the ways they try and ignore it?

2. What is the Scriptural basis for the reality of hell as laid out in this chapter?

3. Why do unbelievers attempt to use the reality of hell as an argument against God's love? How would you respond to someone who said, "God can't exist and be a loving God, if there is a hell?"

4. Why is it important that we not shy away from telling others about the reality of hell?

5. What do universalists believe? How would you answer someone that was a universalist?

Endnotes

1. The Barna Group, "Born Again Christians," http://www.barna.org/FlexPage.aspx?Page-Topic&TopicID-8 (accessed May 13, 2005).

2. P. Kreeft and R. K. Tacelli, *Handbook of Christian Apologetics* (Downers Grove, IL: InterVarsity, 1994), 282.

3. A. Mohler, "Modern Theology: The Disappearance of Hell," in *Hell Under Fire*, ed. C. W. Morgan and R. A. Peterson (Grand Rapids: Zondervan, 2004), 23.

4. W. H. Kimnach, K. P. Minkema, D. A. Sweeney, eds., *The Sermons of Jonathan Edwards* (New Haven: CT, Yale University, 1999), 54–55.

5. R. W. Yarbrough, "Jesus on Hell," in *Hell Under Fire*, 79.

6. Ibid., 80.

7. Ibid., 82.

8. Kreeft and Tacelli, *Handbook of Christian Apologetics*, 287.

9. D. L. Edwards and J. R. W. Stott, *Evangelical Essentials: A Liberal-Evangelical Dialogue* (Downers Grove, IL: InterVarsity, 1988), 314.

10. Yarbrough, "Jesus on Hell," 88.

11. S. W. Ladd, "The Problems of Evil/The Free Will Defense," lecture notes, History of Ideas Class, Southeastern Baptist Theological Seminary, March 2007.

12. Kreeft and Tacelli, *Handbook of Christian Apologetics*, 284.

13. Ibid., 283.

14. D. P. Nelson, "The Work of God: Creation and Providence," in *A Theology for the Church*, ed. D. L. Akin (Nashville: B&H: 2007), 242–92.

15. R. A. Peterson, "Systematic Theology: Three Vantage Points of Hell," 160.

16. C. S. Lewis, *The Abolition of Man* (New York: Macmillan, 1947), 69.

17. Ibid., 127.

18. C. S. Lewis, *The Great Divorce* (New York: Macmillan, 1946), 72.

19. C. S. Lewis, *The Problem of Pain* (1940; reprint, New York: Harper, 1996), 119–20, 124–25, 130.

20. J. P. Moreland, quoted in Lee Strobel, *The Case for Christ* (Grand Rapids: Zondervan Pub, 1998), 174.

21. J. Piper, *The Supremacy of God in Preaching* (Grand Rapids, MI: Baker Books, 2005), 92 .

22. T. Carter, *2200 Quotations from the Writings of J. A. Motyer*, "Hell," in *Baker's Dictionary of Theology*, ed. E. F. Harrison (Grand Rapids: Baker, 1960), 267.

23. W. E. Vine, *An Expository Dictionary of New Testament Words* (McLean, VA: MacDonald, n.d.), 553.

24. Ibid.

Chapter 9

Must a Person Believe in Jesus or Make Him Lord of His Life to Be Saved?

by Elmer Towns

Christians seem to disagree on the process by which people are born again, but they do not disagree on who saves or the basis of salvation. While both groups agree that Jesus is the only Savior from sin, and that the gospel demands belief in the death, burial, and resurrection of Jesus Christ for a person to be saved, they tend to disagree on the process one should follow to be saved.

One group's focus has been referred to as "easy-believism"[1] and maintains that simple faith and trust in Jesus Christ will save. For example when the thief on the cross cried out, "Jesus, remember me when You come into Your kingdom!" (Luke 23:42), Jesus responded, "Today you will be with Me in paradise" (v. 43). Obviously simple faith guaranteed the thief's salvation.

A second group's focus is called "lordship salvation,"[2] which is the view that a person is not saved simply by calling on Jesus. Advocates of this view note that Jesus called people to "repent" (Matt 4:17) and to make a total commitment to discipleship. "If anyone wants to come with Me, he must deny himself, take up his cross daily, and follow Me" (Luke 9:23).

Lordship salvation emphasizes that a person must submit to Christ as Lord over his life, as he trusts Christ for salvation. This view focuses on a changed life that results in salvation. Those who believe in lordship salvation think that a person is not saved if he does not evidence good works in his life. Because the Bible teaches that the life of a believer is changed (2 Cor 5:17), those without fruit, it is argued, are probably not saved (Matt 7:21–23).

Two Contrasting Examples

The contrast between "easy-believism" and "lordship salvation" is seen in the conversions of my wife, Ruth, and me. Our different home backgrounds caused us to come to Christ differently, yet the fact we both came to Christ is evident from our walk with Christ after our salvation experiences.

When Ruth was five years old in a Sunday school class at her home church, the teacher used a wordless book. Showing the first page, which was black, the teacher explained, "Every time you disobey your mother, you put a black stain of sin on your heart." Ruth knew she had disobeyed and the thought of a black heart made a strong impression. Next, the teacher showed the red page and explained, "The blood of Jesus Christ cleanses from all sin; it washes away any black stain in your heart." The next page was white. "You can have a white heart, with your sins forgiven," the teacher explained. Ruth wanted the blood of Jesus to cleanse her from sin. The next page was gold, to reflect the gold streets of heaven where she would go at death. Then the green page reflected growth, which God expects of new Christians.[3] That day the teacher led Ruth to pray for Jesus to come into her heart. She did, and Ruth has lived for God ever since that experience. If that's easy-believism, it works!

My conversion was difficult. My mother had met my father at a dance, and I grew up in a house with an alcoholic father and an angry mother. A door-to-door coffee salesman took me to Sunday school when I entered the first grade, and I never missed a Sunday for 14 years. On Easter Sunday, 1944, I joined the church along with about a dozen other children my age. The pastor asked each of us a theological question, then he asked the rest of us if we too "believed" that point. I think my belief was a simple mental agreement.

The pastor asked Frank Perry, the last boy in the line, if he believed Jesus was coming back to earth. Frank said, "Yes," and I agreed, along with the rest of the young people. But the thought of Jesus coming scared me. I "accepted the fact" that Jesus was coming back to earth, but I knew I was not ready to meet Him.

So, throughout junior high and senior high school, I must have prayed dozens of times, "Lord, save me" or "Lord Jesus, come into my heart." But even after those prayers, I knew I was lost and I knew I was not ready to meet the Lord.

In the summer of 1950 three students from Columbia Bible College conducted a revival meeting at a mission church outside of Savannah, Georgia, my hometown. Revival swept the little community of Bonna Bella; five or six people were converted each night for a week and a half. Then on July 25, 1950, no one came forward. Bill Harding stepped down beside the communion table to announce, "Someone here is breaking the revival; you're holding on to that pew and won't let go." I looked down to see my fingers tightly clutching the back of the pew. Instantly I snatched my hands away.

Bill instructed, "Go home . . . kneel by your bed . . . look into heaven . . . tell God, 'Jesus, come into my heart and save me.'"

I said inwardly, "I'll do it."

About 11:15 that night I knelt by my bed, looked into heaven, and I told God, "I've prayed that prayer many times, but it doesn't work." I had been riding my bike delivering papers and cried out loud many times, "Lord, save me." But nothing had ever happened.

That night I prayed the Lord's Prayer—very seriously—emphasizing, "Forgive us our trespasses." Then I hopped into bed, but still felt lost. I tossed and turned and could not go to sleep. I did not realize both God and the devil were wrestling for my soul. I was still hanging on to my old life and all the habits I thought were sin.

After a few minutes I got on my knees again. I looked in heaven and began the prayer, only to say again, "It doesn't work." But I didn't want to go to hell, so I prayed very seriously,

Now I lay me
Down to sleep.
I pray Thee Lord
My soul to keep.
If I should die
Before I wake,
I pray Thee, Lord,
My soul to take.

I emphasized that last part several times, "I pray Thee, Lord, my soul to take." Then I climbed back into bed, only to continue tossing and turning. It was a hot night and I perspired—not so much from the summer heat but from my built-up conviction.

I knew I had to surrender everything to the Lord. When I could not stand the pressure any longer, I knelt by my bed, looked into heaven and I prayed, "Lord Jesus, come into my heart and save me." I instantly surrendered all! Whereas those words had never worked previously, this time I experienced an inner explosion of joy and peace and a thrill I had never felt. I knew Jesus had come into my life and I knew I was saved, just as surely as a previously blind man knows light when he sees it for the first time.

I leaped to my feet. My struggle was conquered by faith and I fist pumped in the dark room. I began singing these triumphant words inwardly,

> *Amazing grace, how sweet the sound*
> *That saved a wretch like me!*
> *I once was lost, but now am found;*
> *Was blind, but now I see.*

For me, it was lordship salvation. I gave Jesus everything including my desires, my sins, and my life's goals. Immediately I knew I was called of God into full-time Christian service. I was not sure then what that would mean, but whatever God wanted me to do, I was ready to do it with all my strength.

Easy-Believism

Point

- Definition: Easy-believism is called free grace or a faith position whereby a person calls on Jesus Christ to save him or her. Key Verse: "Believe on the Lord Jesus Christ and you will be saved" (Acts 16:31).
- Key Illustration: The thief on the cross who cried, "Remember me when You come into Your kingdom" (Luke 23:42). Jesus replied, "Today you will be with Me in paradise" (v. 43).

The easy-believism position is almost never called that by its proponents. Some adherents have called it non-lordship salvation, or "free grace."[4]

Those who hold to "faith alone" say that belief means more than mental knowledge or intellectual assent. They see belief as complete reliance on another person, that is, on Jesus Christ. The illustration is given of a person who knows an airplane can get off the ground and fly safely, but he refuses to enter the plane out of fear, or he is psychologically inhibited or has some other emotional "block." So he refuses to board the plane. But when a person knows an airplane can fly and he commits himself to fly by entering the plane and buckling himself into a seat, that person illustrates believing faith in Christ for salvation. This is what Paul meant when he referred to "the obedience of faith" (Rom 1:5) or "you obeyed from the heart" (6:17).

Those who hold easy-believism ask the question, "What would 'hard-believism' look like?" They also ask, "How could anyone make believing harder?"[5] As Bernie L. Gillespie wrote, "To have faith means more than to have an opinion, belief or conviction. It means far more than knowledge or acknowledgment. It means trust and reliance."[6]

Counterpoint

- Easy-believism produces "cheap grace" that waters down the gospel to anyone who prays for salvation without turning his entire life over to Jesus Christ.
- Weak churches are filled with professing Christians who have not experienced the power of God in their lives.
- Easy-believism gives a false assurance to those who only make a "Christian" decision, but are not born again.

- Easy-believism emphasizes decisionism, numerical success, and church "bigness" for the sake of growth.
- Easy-believism grows out of a wrong motivation for evangelism.

1. *Easy-believism produces "cheap grace" that waters down the gospel to those who pray for salvation without turning their entire lives over to Jesus Christ.*

Arthur Pink, a theologian of a previous generation, stated this about easy-believism: "The way of salvation is falsely defined. In most instances the modern 'evangelist' assures his congregation that all any sinner has to do in order to escape hell and make sure of heaven is to 'receive Christ as his personal Savior.' But such teaching is utterly misleading. No one can receive Christ as his Savior while he rejects Him as Lord!"[7]

Dietrich Bonhoeffer in his classic book, *The Cost of Discipleship,* described easy-believism as cheap grace.

> Cheap grace is the deadly enemy of our Church. We are fighting today for costly grace. . . . Cheap grace is the preaching of forgiveness without requiring repentance, baptism without church discipline, communion without confession. . . . Cheap grace is grace without discipleship, grace without the cross, grace without Jesus Christ living and incarnate.[8]

2. *Weak churches are filled with professing Christians who have not experienced the power of God in their lives or ministry.*

Some have accused easy-believism as the reason so many churches today are powerless. Josh Buice says of the Southern Baptist Convention, "The gimmick of 'Easy-Believism' has been utilized to puff up our numbers—and the results are weak and ineffective churches."[9] Then Buice asks two questions: "Could it be that our SBC churches are in a state of decline because of the easy-believism message that has been spewed from the pulpits for decades? Could it be that our church roles are bloated with non-attendees and unregenerate membership?"[10]

3. Easy-believism gives a false assurance to those who made a "Christian" decision, but were not born again.

R. L. Hymers Jr. and Christopher Cagan call easy-believism "decisionism," and they say those who make such decisions are not saved. "Conversion is from God. Decisionism is from man. In decisionism a person does something which takes the place of a saving encounter with Jesus but is, in fact, not that at all. That is why so many people are unsaved today."[11]

4. Easy-believism emphasizes decisionism, numerical success, and church "bigness" for the sake of growth.

Hymers and Cagan define decisionism in this way:

> Decisionism is the belief that a person is saved by com-
> ing forward, raising the hand, saying a prayer, believing
> a doctrine . . . or some other external, human act, which
> is taken as the equivalent to, and proof of, the miracle of
> inward conversion. . . . Decisionism is purely human, car-
> nal, and natural.[12]

Easy-believism is also called "easy prayerism." David Cloud states,

Easy prayerism . . . is a methodology which focuses on getting people to say a prayer. . . . What I am against is making this the focus of our evangelistic activity. Repeating a prayer is not necessarily salvation, and we must not confuse it with such.[13]

Mark Finkbeiner also associates easy-believism with the contemporary emphasis on bigness.

Easy believism . . . retards Christian growth. This is how many liberal, compromising Christians get their big numbers. They try to make everyone feel comfortable in their sin and then they brag about their big numbers that they claim to have converted.[14]

Keith Green calls those preachers "fools" for using easy-believism techniques.

Can't you see what fools we are? We preach a man-made, plastic gospel. We get people to come forward to "the altar" by bringing psychological pressures that have nothing to do with God. We "lead them" in a prayer that they are not yet convinced they need to say. And then to top it all off, we give them "counseling," telling them it is a sin to doubt that they're really saved![15]

5. *Easy-believism grows out of wrong motivation for evangelism.*

Again Josh Buice attacks easy-believism in these words: "The average [Southern] Baptist church has long rested upon a foundation of numerical success. The success of most SBC churches is directly related to the report given at the end of the local association's yearly report with the line item heading – 'Total Baptisms.'"[16] Then Buice concludes, "The message of easy-believism + numerical success needs to be rejected and considered an enemy of the church!"[17]

Lordship Salvation

Point

- *Definition:* "Lordship salvation is the position that receiving Christ involves a turning in the heart from sin and, as a part of faith, a submissive commitment to obey Jesus Christ as Lord. It also maintains that progressive *sanctification* and perseverance must necessarily follow conversion. Those who hold to the doctrine of *perseverance of the saints* see this not only as a requirement, but an assured certainty according to the sustaining grace of Christ."[18]

- Key Verse: "If anyone wants to come with Me, he must deny himself, take up his cross daily, and follow Me" (Luke 9:23).

- Key Illustration: The Rich Young Ruler (Luke 18:18–24). "A ruler asked Him, 'Good Teacher, what must I do to inherit eternal life?' 'Why do you call Me good?' Jesus asked him. 'No one is good but One—God. You know the commandments: Do not commit adultery; do not murder; do not steal; do not bear false witness; honor your father and mother.' 'I have kept all these from my youth,' he said. When Jesus heard this, He told him, 'You still lack one thing: sell all that you have and distribute it to the poor, and you will have treasure in heaven. Then come, follow Me.' After he heard this, he became extremely sad, because he was very rich. Seeing that he became sad, Jesus said, 'How hard it is for those who have wealth to enter the kingdom of God!'"

Counterpoint

- Lordship salvation is based on or includes works, which do not save.
- Lordship salvation confuses the call to salvation with the call to discipleship.
- Lordship salvation is like a return to Roman Catholicism, sacerdotalism, or denominations that include works for salvation.
- Lordship salvation is contrary to the open arms of God and the free offer of salvation.
- Lordship salvation has a "fixation" on repentance found in the Synoptic Gospels, while under-emphasizing grace found in the Gospel of John and the Epistles.

The power of the gospel (Rom 1:16) is that it not only forgives a person of his sins; it also transforms the sinner into a new creation in Christ Jesus (2 Cor 5:17). Many who hold the lordship view believe many Christians lack obedience because they were not properly introduced to Christ (i.e., they did not really get saved).

The lordship position believes Jesus cannot be considered a person's Savior without being his Lord. This suggests that a sinner must have a radical turning from sin when he believes in Christ.

Therefore lordship salvation proponents say a new believer will reflect progressive sanctification. Those who hold to the perseverance of the saints believe that those who are truly born again and continue to live the Christian life will gain heaven.

When a person accepts Christ, he also accepts Him as Lord. Many point to Rom 10:9 to support the lordship view of salvation. "If you confess with your mouth, 'Jesus is Lord,' and believe in your heart that God raised Him from the dead, you will be saved."

Also when a person is converted, he must count the cost. This includes carrying one's cross. "If anyone wants to come with Me, he must deny himself, take up his cross daily, and follow Me" (Luke 9:23). Lordship salvation proponents also point to other verses that suggest counting the cost: Luke 9:57–62; 14:26–27; Rom 13:14. This idea of counting the cost is associated with repenting. A person looks at both sides of the issues, weighs the options, and then chooses to follow Jesus Christ.

1. Lordship salvation is based on or includes works which do not save.

Those who renounce lordship salvation point to Eph 2:8–9. "For by grace you are saved through faith, and this is not from yourselves; it is God's gift—not from works, so that no one can boast." They emphasize the phrase "not from works," and they conclude that anything that is viewed as necessary for a person to do to be saved is works.

If "works" are added to salvation, then the biblical meaning on faith and justification is destroyed. People are saved by faith alone apart from keeping the law. "For we conclude that a man is justified by faith apart from works of law" (Rom 3:28). This is *sola fide*, "by faith alone," the cry of the Reformation.

2. Lordship salvation confuses the call to salvation with the call to discipleship.

Stephen Olford says this of the lordship salvation view: "There was no 'easy-believism' in Paul's presentation of the Gospel. Decision was to be accompanied and followed by devotion. Jesus Christ IS Lord and, therefore, MUST be Lord in our lives."[19]

Discipleship or following Jesus is good and desirable, but it is not the same as becoming a Christian. A disciple is one who followed Jesus (even some of Jesus' earthly disciples were not true and faithful (John 6:66). Then disciples were later called Christians (Acts 11:26).

In becoming a Christian a person receives a new nature. He is justified (declared perfect) before the Father, and the Holy Spirit comes to dwell in his life. The disciples who followed Jesus in His earthly ministry did not have these advantages. A born-again believer has so much more today than a disciple who followed Jesus on this earth. Therefore pre-cross qualifications should not be added to His post-cross ministry.

How can salvation be a free gift if one must repent, be a disciple, or do any other such thing? Lordship salvation minimizes the up-front relationship with Christ by demanding the final results of walking with Christ, bearing spiritual fruit, and being committed to Christ. Some apparently promote lordship salvation because of their concern that some people claim to be Christians, but do not live for Christ.

3. Lordship salvation is like a return to Roman Catholicism, sacerdotalism, or denominations that include works for salvation.

Christian N. Temple states that lordship salvation is a return to the pre-Reformation days.

In time, the rise of legalism, sacerdotalism, and Roman Catholicism, and other heresies were to introduce into Christianity many paganistic works-toward-salvation doctrines, but the true church of regenerate believers would hold solidly to the teachings of the Lord and the Apostles. . . . As the Protestant Reformers separated from the Roman church, their rallying cry was that of Sola Fide, faith Alone! The same doctrine has been a cornerstone for conservative Protestant churches ever since that time.[20]

While the above argument is guilt by association, it also is an attempt to point out the uniqueness of the grace position as opposed to the "works" position. Ever since Cain, people have tried to substitute the work of their hands to please God. But God always relates to people by grace through faith.

4. Lordship salvation is contrary to the open arms of God and the free offer of salvation.

The Bible pictures God who loves the world so much that He sent His son to die for the sins of mankind (John 1:29; 3:16). "God did not send His Son into the world that He might condemn the world, but that the world might be saved through Him" (John 3:17). He is "patient with you, not wanting any to perish" (2 Pet 3:9). These verses picture God's longing heart for sinners to come to Him. They are a picture of the father of the prodigal son, "But while the son was still a long way off, his father saw him and was filled with compassion. He ran, threw his arms around his neck, and kissed him" (Luke 15:20). That is a picture of the heavenly Father who loves prodigals and is waiting for them to return to Him. Luke 15:10 states, "There is joy in the presence of God's angels over one sinner who repents."

5. *Lordship salvation has a fixation on repentance found in the Synoptic Gospels, while underemphasizing grace found in the Gospel of John and the Epistles.*

The *Wikipedia Encyclopedia* states, "Free Grace theology claims that the Lordship position is 'fixated' on the works-minded Gospel of Matthew while overlooking the Grace-minded Gospel of John."[21]

The word *repent* is not found in the Gospel of John, which reflects the emphasis of grace. And the word *belief* occurs 98 times in John's Gospel. The word belief was so strong and compelling that the word repent was not needed to explain the simplicity of the gospel.

Wrap-Up

Unfortunately both sides think they are right, and each one accuses the other of not being biblical.[22]

The two extremes may represent how different people respond to the gospel. Since God reaches people where they are, different methods may be needed to reach people who come from different backgrounds or with varying degrees of sin. And it takes a different approach to reach someone who has no awareness of God, compared with one who is close to salvation, as measured on the Engle Scale.[23]

Faith is not measured by sincerity. The strength of one's faith is measured by the strength of Christ, and the integrity of one's faith is measured by focusing faith on Christ. Faith is stepping into the waiting arms of Christ, but the place from which each person steps may differ (different cultures, needs, pressures, and backgrounds).

Perhaps the illustration of a door can help bring both sides together. On the front side of the door is Christ's invitation,

"Come to Me" (Matt 11:28). This side represents what the sinner must do. The back side of the door is regeneration (John 3:3–7) and justification (Rom 5:1). This side of the door represents what God does in saving a sinner. When the believing sinner does his part, he pushes the door open. Then God works from the other side, and gives the believing sinner a new nature and declares him righteous before God (i.e., he is justified).

The gospel is at the heart of those who take either side in this issue. "I want to clarify for you the gospel . . . that Christ died for our sins . . . that He was buried, that He was raised on the third day according to the Scriptures" (1 Cor 15:1–4). Both sides emphasize the death, burial, and resurrection of Christ. When both sides agree on the gospel, that is good.

But even though both sides disagree, people are finding Christ by the efforts of both sides. Both sides pray for lost people to be saved, both sides preach the gospel, and both sides make sincere efforts to get people saved, and that is commendable.

DISCUSSION QUESTIONS

1. Why are some Christians so critical of those who hold and practice a position different from theirs on how to become a Christian?

2. What should be one's attitude toward those who hold the opposite view of becoming a Christian? Why?

3. Is either extreme right, or is the proper approach to salvation halfway between the two positions? Why?

4. Is there any relationship between a person's spiritual gift and how he views a person must be saved?

5. What is there in one's religious background (or no religious influence) that influences how he says a person must come to salvation?

Endnotes

1. "Free Grace Theology," *Wikipedia Encyclopedia*, at http://en.wikipedia.org/wiki/Free_Grace_theology (accessed August 13, 2010).

2. "Lordship Salvation," *Wikipedia Encyclopedia*, at http://en.wikipedia.org/wiki/Lordship_salvation (accessed August 13, 2010).

3. *KIDOLOGY, "Equipping and Encouraging Those Who Minister to Children,"* http://www.kidology.org/zones/zone_post.asp?post_id=120 (accessed August 9, 2010).

4. "Lordship Salvation," *Theopedia,* http://www.theopedia.com/Lordship_salvation (accessed August 9, 2010).

5. B. L. Gillespie, "Easy Believism: How Would 'Hard Believism' Affect the Gospel?" *ICA In Christ Alone!* available at http://inchristalone.org/Easy%20Believism.pdf (accessed August 9, 2010).

6. Ibid.

7. A. W. Pink, *Present-day Evangelism* (Miffinburg, PA: Bible Truth, 1958). See also T. Williamson, "Case Studies in Easy-Believism," http://www.rogershermansociety.org/easy-believism2.htm (accessed August 9, 2010).

8. F. Fritz, "Beyond Easy Believism!" SermonCentral.com, http://www.sermoncentral.com/Sermons/SearchResults.asp?Keyword=BEYOND+EASY+BELIEVISM%21 (accessed August 9, 2010).

9. J. Buice, "Easy-Believism + Numbers: The Unmistakable Link" Grace Christian Blog and Articles available at http://www.delivered-bygrace.com/?p-1050 (accessed August 9, 2010).

10. Ibid.

11. Williamson, "Case Studies in Easy-Believism."

12. Ibid.

13. Ibid.

14. Ibid.

15. Ibid.

16. Ibid.

17. Ibid.

18. "Lordship Salvation," *Theopedia (italics his)*.

19. "Easy-Believism + Numbers: The Unmistakable Link," Grace Christian Blog and Articles.

20. C. N. Temple, "Lordship Salvation: Is It Biblical?" Darkness to Light, http://www.dtl.org/salvation/article/guest/lordship-1.htm (accessed August 10, 2010).

21. *Wikipedia Encyclopedia*, "Lordship Salvation."

22. The following three Web sites include articles attacking easy-believism: (1) "Apologist: Youths Need Truth Not Easy Believism," *Christian Post*, http://www.christianpost.com/article/20100120/apologist-youths-need-truth-not-easy-believism/index.html; Mike Ratliff, "The Abomination of Easy-Believism—Part 4—The Real God of the Bible," *Possessing the Treasure* at http://mikeratliff.wordpress.com/2008/08/21/the-abomination-of-easy-believism-part-4-the-real-god-of-the-bible; and Midway Bible Baptist Church, Fishersville, Virginia, "Identifying Easy-Believism," *Provoking Thoughts*, http://www.midwaybiblebaptistchurch.com/prov-thot/pt15.htm#identify.

The following three Web sites contain articles attacking lordship salvation: J. W. Robbins, "The Gospel according to John MacArthur," *Trinity Foundation*, http://www.trinityfoundation.org/journal.php?id-193; M. J. Sawyer, "Some Thoughts on Lordship Salvation," *Bible.org*, http://bible.org/article/some-thoughts-lordship-salvation; and D. J. Stewart, "Lordship Salvation Ignores Babes in Christ and the Backslidden," http://www.jesus-is-savior.com/False%20Doctrines/Lordship%20Salvation/ignores.htm.

23. The Engle Scale is a spiritual measurement of individuals that determines their "spiritual readiness" to become Christians and measures the spiritual process needed to bring a person to salvation. Engle gives eight "stations," from the farthest, the person who does not accept the existence of God, to the closest, the person who knows the gospel and is ready for salvation. The scale is called a "Spiritual Decision Process Model." It examines the "process" of becoming a Christian (E. Towns, ed., *A Practical Encyclopedia of Evangelism and Church Growth* [Ventura, CA: Regal, 1995], 197).

Chapter 10

How Detailed Is God's Wonderful Plan for Each Individual Life?

by Elmer Towns

God's will for my life became a crisis in my first year of college. One day I sat in chapel contemplating what the speaker said, "Young people, the thing you don't want to do is God's will for your life." The speaker was pleading for us to surrender our lives to God's will, and then do it. Then he said something like this, "If you don't want to go to Africa as a missionary, that's the thing God wants you to do. Surrender. . . ."

I was willing to do anything God wanted me to do, so Africa was not a problem for me. Then the missionary went on to say, "If you don't want to study linguistics because it is too hard for you, and the challenge of breaking down a native language into an alphabet scares you and you don't want to do it, then that's God's will for your life."

I thought that learning a language would be a wonderful thing to do, so linguistics was not a challenge for me.

But I turned my head to see a girl that was rather large. She obviously was not listening to the sermon; she was fiddling with her purse. I remembered this girl did not have a heart for spiritual things, so I had never been interested in her. It never even crossed my mind to ask her for a date. Then the missionary interrupted my thoughts, "The thing you don't want to do is God's will for your life."

"I don't want to marry that girl," crossed my mind.

Just about the time he again challenged us to do what we did not want to do; that girl popped into my mind.

"*Oh, no . . .*" I thought to myself. "*I'd hate to marry her.*"

For the next couple of weeks I could not get the thought of marrying that girl out of my mind. Even though she was not spiritual, I wondered if God was telling me to marry her and make her spiritual. I was almost afraid to pray, knowing an image of that girl would pop into my mind, and I did not want anything to do with her. Then I would hear the missionary say again, "Surrender . . . what you don't want to do is God's will for your life."

Approximately two weeks later a lady missionary from South America spoke in chapel. She told her life's story of always wanting to go to the mission field, always wanting to go to South America, of always wanting to minister among the tribes of people who had never heard the name of Jesus. Then this lady said, "The thing you want to do more than anything else in life, is God's will for you."

"Wow! What a great relief!" That day the Holy Spirit took off my shoulders the weight of doing His will. I then realized that the issue is being yielded to God. If a believer is yielded to God, what he wants to do is probably God's will. However, if he is not yielded to God, if he is fighting Him, then what he does not want to do is probably God's will.

The following summer God gave me another insight into the will of God. I had worked in a Christian camp for $5 a week, and so at the end of the month I had only $20 in my pocket from four weeks of work. I was in downtown Savannah, Georgia, shopping for some new shirts to return to Columbia Bible College in my second year. I was in the bargain basement of W. T. Grant's, looking over a large bin of shirts marked 88 cents each. Since money came hard, I did not want to make a poor choice, so I compared the shirts for a long time. Thinking no one was watching, I bowed my head to pray, "God, which shirts should I buy?"

When I opened my eyes, I was shocked to see a face staring up at me. Ardell, a fellow camp counselor, had seen what I was doing. He stuck his head under my bent-over face and looked straight up at me. When I opened my eyes I was startled.

"What are you doing?" Ardell asked me.

Obviously, I had to confess, "I was praying about which shirt I should buy."

"I knew it," he said, almost dancing a jig because he knew he was right.

"You're too spiritual," he barked at me. By that he meant I let my feelings guide my life. Then he continued, "You don't pray about shirts; you pick your size, then you pick the right color to fit with trousers and jackets, then pick a shirt that appeals to you; but you don't pray about little things like which shirts to buy."

I believed Ardell. From then on, I began to find the will of God in little decisions through common sense. But I continued to pray about the big decisions in life, those life-turning decisions. But small things I left to common sense.

Then when I went to the store I did not pray over whether I should buy vegetable soup or beef barley; I bought what I liked and needed. That approach has applied to most of my life.

Sixty years later Ardell phoned me about another matter and we talked about the situation of the shirts. Apparently the incident made as big an impression on him as on me. He commented that I became more practical in life, and over time he became more spiritual in seeking God's will for his life.

Bill Bright, founder and first president of Campus Crusade for Christ, came to know Christ when someone told him, "God loves you, and has a wonderful plan for your life."[1]

That part about God having a "wonderful plan" for his life intrigued Bill. He believed in Christ, and then determined to find God's "wonderful plan" and do it.

Suppose God had a "wonderful plan" for you to be an engineer? Does God's plan include what university you should attend? Is God's plan so specific that it includes whether you take electrical engineering, structural engineering, or architectural engineering? Does God's "wonderful plan" involve which courses you should take, which books to read, whether you should take notes on a legal pad or an I-pad? Does God's "wonderful plan" include the firm where you work or even what desk where you will sit? How specific is God's "wonderful plan for your life?"

Maybe God's plan for your life includes just the occupation, and even a specific area within your occupation such as highway bridge engineering. But God leaves details to you, that is, study habits, friendships within your occupation, work habits, and the type of engineering instruments you purchase and use.

Although Paul did not state how specific God's will is, he encouraged believers to be smart and learn God's will for their lives. "So don't be foolish, but understand what the Lord's will is" (Eph 5:17).

Because God knows everything and has the power to direct everything, how can believers not believe that He does not have a perfect, predetermined plan for each of His followers? Would an all-wise God create a world in which He did not know what was going to happen? Can an all-powerful God be surprised at what His creatures do? Because Christians believe in an infinite, all-powerful, and all-knowing God, they must believe He controls everything in His universe.

In one sense God is never surprised by anything Christians do. The fact that God is eternal means He is without beginning and without end. There is no yesterday or tomorrow with God, nor is there a next year, or a next decade. God now stands at every point in individuals' lives so that He knows everything they have done in the past, and will do in the future. Nothing catches Him by surprise.

Somewhere between the freedom of man to make choices, which includes the freedom to fail or succeed, and God's sovereignty is God's work of predestination. God is sovereign and God controls everything that comes to pass. No one can understand how God does it. How can God control the outcome of every situation, and yet allow His creatures freedom to carry out their own will?

The Scriptures hold up both, that man is free, and that God controls everything. These can never be reconciled because people are finite. But God understands this reconciliation perfectly because He is infinite. "Oh, what a wonderful God we have! How great are his wisdom and knowledge . . . . How impossible it is for us to understand his decisions and his methods!" (Rom 11:33 LB).

God's Will Is a Perfect, Preplanned Design for Your Life

Point

- Definition: God's Will of Decree or Sovereign Will — "The will of God refers . . . to God having a plan for humanity and as such desires to see such plan fulfilled."[9]
- Key Verse: "My Father! If it is possible, let this cup pass from Me. Yet not as I will, but as You will" (Matt 26:39).
- Key Illustration: Jesus submitted to the Father's divine plan to die for the sins of the world.

A perfect preplanned will for your life does not consider man's sin and rebellion. How can someone go back to marry the perfect spouse he rejected when he was out of the will of God? Both that person and the "perfect" spouse may already be married to another. Any plan for a person's life must consider the "permissive will of God." God does not force His sinful children into His perfect will. Instead He guides them through an imperfect world to live a life of victory for His glory.

Counterpoint

- There are no perfect pre-plans by God because any sin or rebellion by a Christian would destroy a perfect plan or invalidate it.
- If God had a perfect pre-plan for a believer's life, that would take away their free will and make them robots in their response to God.
- A perfect predetermined plan takes away internal motives to love and worship God, and probably destroys any incentive to serve Him.

• A perfect pre-planned life is contrary to God's purpose in the original creation of Adam and Eve and His continuing relationship with people throughout the Bible.

1. *There are no perfect pre-plans by God because any sin or rebellion by a Christian would destroy the perfect plan or invalidate it.*

If God had one perfect spouse for a person, but he rebelled against God and married someone else, what would happen to the rest of God's preplan for his life? What happens if the one he was supposed to marry marries someone else? To get back into the perfect will of God, must both persons get a divorce? How could that be in the will of God? Paul discussed the situation in which a believer is married to an unbeliever, and he told them to stay in that marriage, "Each person should remain in the life situation in which he was called" (1 Cor 7:20). Paul was suggesting that a person cannot fix this problem by a divorce.

Perhaps there is no way anyone could stay in the perfect will of God—if the will of God is a pre-drawn blueprint.

Dietrich Bonhoeffer was a Christian minister who rebelled against Adolph Hitler in pre-World War II Germany. Bonhoeffer was part of a failed conspiracy to murder Hitler. Can murder be in the will of God? Bonhoeffer was hanged by the Nazis, yet he wrote this about God's will.

The will of God is not a system of rules established from the outset. It is something new and different in each different situation in life. And for this reason a man must forever reexamine what the will of God may be. The will of God may lie deeply concealed beneath a great number of possibilities.[2]

2. If God had a perfect plan for a believer's life, that would take away from their free will and make them robots in their response to God.

The command to "love the Lord your God with all your heart" (Matt 22:37; cp. Deut. 6:5) expresses God's desire for each believer. But that command suggests there are times when a believer may not love God with all his heart, or that he loves the Lord less than he should. So what does that mean? Since Christians are not perfect they would never measure up to a perfect pre-drawn blueprint for their lives.

That leads to another question: Could a perfect God draw a less-than-perfect blueprint for people who will never be perfect?" The answer is, Probably not! Every exhortation by God for believers to press on to perfection is an argument for their free will. Paul prayed that the Colossians may "stand mature" (Col 4:12), and he wanted the Thessalonians to "complete what is lacking in [their] faith" (1 Thess 3:10).

Every exhortation to yield to God recognizes how far short one's free will falls from God's perfect will. "I plead with you to give your bodies to God. . . . Don't copy the behavior and customs of this world, but let God transform you into a new person by changing the way you think. Then you will know what God wants for you to do, and you will know how good and pleasing and perfect his will really is" (Rom 12:1–2 NLT). These verses hold out the promise that believers can know and do God's perfect will, even when they are far short of it.

The fact that people have a free will that many times acts contrary to God's perfect will suggests there is no perfect plan for their lives.

3. A perfect pre-determined plan takes away internal motives to love and worship God, and probably destroys any incentive to serve Him.

The doctrine of crowns motivates believers to strive for excellence. Rewards are an argument for free will and an argument against any pre-drawn blueprint for our lives. Paul wrote that "Satan hindered us," but he pressed on in evangelism for converts who became his "glory and joy" (1 Thess 2:18–19).

Rewards are earned by faithfulness and good works. "If anyone's work that he has built survives, he will receive a reward" (1 Cor 3:14). While salvation is a free gift (Eph 2:8–9), believers are to strive for rewards (Matt 10:42; 1 Cor 9:24–25; 2 Tim 4:7–8; Rev 22:12).

The fact that God the Father wants people to worship Him (John 4:23), suggest that no one worships God as much as he should, nor as deeply as he should. God wants worship from those who choose to praise Him out of grateful hearts, not out of constraint or forced allegiance. A pre-drawn blueprint does not allow for freedom of choice.

4. A perfect pre-planned life is contrary to God's purpose in the original creation of Adam and Eve and His continuing relationship with people throughout the Bible.

God gave Adam and Eve a command to "Be fruitful, multiply, fill the earth, and subdue it" (Gen 1:28). Then God gave them freedom "to eat from any tree of the garden" (2:16). God did not tell them when to eat, where to eat, what fruit to eat, or how much to eat. He gave them freedom in their independence Yes. He expected obedience. "But you must not eat from the tree of the knowledge of good and evil" (v. 17). To emphasize the nature of freedom, God warned that disobedience would be costly, "for on the day you eat from it, you will certainly die" (v. 17).

God's Will Is Guidance

Point

- Definition: This is sometimes called, "God's will of command." God's will is an extension of His power of choice, so that He guides individuals to conform to His commands or standards.[3]
- Key Verse: "Give thanks in everything, for this is God's will for you in Christ Jesus" (1 Thess 5:18).
- Key Illustration: God guided Paul through the Mediterranean Sea from the Holy Land to Rome, including dangers, setbacks, answers to prayer, and victorious deliverances (Acts 27).

Counterpoint

God knows all things, and has all power to direct His children to fulfill the purposes He has for them, and He loves them and wants the best for them. Therefore why would He not have an all-inclusive pre-plan for each of those He created?

- To deny God's ability to work His perfect plan for believers' lives denies His all-knowing and all-powerful ability to do what He pleases.
- Because the eternal God is living now at the point of every success or failure, He can fashion a perfect preplan that

includes victories over barriers and His forgiveness when one fails.

• Because God works in believers both to will and to do His plan, He can fashion His plan and motivate them to do His will.

• Because there are illustrations in Scripture that reflect God's control over people to work details according to His preplan.

1. *To deny God's ability to work His perfect plan for believers' lives denies His all-knowing and all-powerful ability to do what He pleases.*

John Piper says there are two types of the will of God. The first he calls *God's will of decree*, or God's *sovereign will*. This is His sovereign control over all that comes to pass."[4] This concept of the will of God is different from fate, which is "an event or a course of events that will inevitably happen in the future. Fate is the events that will happen to a person that cannot be changed. Fate is also viewed as an irresistible power or agency that determines the future. It is a concept based on the belief that there is a fixed, natural order to the universe."[5] This concept believes fate resides in an irresistible power or force that controls everything. When bad things happen to good people, it is fate; and the same is true when good things happen to bad people.

Fatalism is depressing, and kills all incentives. Fatalism is not biblical, for a Christian believes in human freedom and that human choice is based on one's responsibility to God. As R. C. Sproul said, "God's sovereign will is often hidden from us until it comes to pass."[6] Therefore, people think they have freedom of choice, but after the event occurs, it is evident that God has accomplished His will.

2. Because the eternal God is living now at the point of every success or failure He can fashion a perfect preplan that includes our victories over barriers and His forgiveness when one fails.

This view says that when a person makes a choice, he thinks he is responsible, but in fact he only perceives it that way. Viewed from God's perspective, He predetermines what people do or choose. He is not limited by time; He created time, which is the distance between the sequences of events. Therefore there is no "preplanning" with God. He simply does His will.

When a Christian thinks he can or cannot do the will of God, he is looking at an event or his reaction to the event, through human eyes; he seldom sees things from a divine perspective.

3. Because God works in believers both to will and to do His plan, He can fashion His plan and motivate them to do His will.

The Scriptures teach that God initiates people to do His will. "For it is God who is working in you, enabling you both to will and to act for His good purpose" (Phil 2:13). Therefore when a person decides to obey God's will, actually God had previously worked in his heart to motivate him to follow His plan.

Some have called this view "providentialism." This is "a belief that God's will is evident in all occurrences. It can further be described as a belief that the power of God (or Providence) is so complete that humans cannot equal His abilities, or fully understand His plan."[7]

People need to understand that "the LORD has prepared everything for His purpose" (Prov 16:4). As Todd Strandberg wrote,

> Because God is the One who set the world in motion, it is logical to assume that He is able to determine the course of events. Whatever outcome He desires will come to pass. If we are to know our own fate, we need to understand what God has decreed for our life.[8]

4. Because there are illustrations in Scripture that reflect God's control over people to work details according to His plan.

"All things work together for the good of those who love God" (Rom 8:28). Does *all things* actually mean everything? Can it mean that God "works events together" when people do not do His will? Why not?

People sometimes say, "The devil is in the details." Why then cannot Christians believe that "God is in the details"?

Paul wrote that God "made known to us the mystery of His will . . . according to the purpose of the One who works out everything in agreement with the decision of His will" (Eph 1:9,11). Rom 8:28 referred to "all things," and here in Eph 1:11 "everything" is mentioned. How interesting to see God work "all things" together to accomplish His will.

Joseph, Jacob's eleventh son, bragged to his brothers about his importance (Gen 37:5–11). The brothers sold Joseph into slavery. But then years later; he became Egypt's Secretary of Agriculture and saved Egypt from complete starvation. Then Joseph said to his brothers, "You planned evil against me; God planned it for good to bring about the present result—the survival of many people"

(Gen 50:20). Did God's will involve only the big events to save Joseph, or did it include many small preplanned events?

When Nebuchadnezzar was humbled by God because of His arrogant claim to have built Babylon, the sovereign plan of God was at work. John Piper said this of this event:

> That's the first meaning of the will of God: it is God's sovereign control of all things. We will call this his "sovereign will" or his "will of decree." It cannot be broken. It always comes to pass. "He does according to *his will* among the host of heaven and among the inhabitants of the earth; and none can stay his hand or say to him, 'What have you done?'" (Dan 4:35 ESV, italics added)[9]

Romans 9:17–18,20–21 speaks of God's sovereign plan:

> "For the Scripture tells Pharaoh: For this reason I raised you up: so that I may display My power in you, and that My name may be proclaimed in all the earth. So then, He shows mercy to whom He wills, and He hardens whom He wills. . . . But who are you—anyone who talks back to God? Will what is formed say to the one who formed it, 'Why did you make me like this?' Or has the potter no right over His clay, to make from the same lump one piece of pottery for honor and another for dishonor?"

Thus it seems that God has predetermined events in the world for His own purpose, even when He judges people. Perhaps He does this because He wants to "display His wrath and to make His power known" (Rom 9:22).

The answer to God's power is found in God Himself. "So then it does not depend on human will or effort, but on God who shows mercy" (Rom 9:16).

Wrap-ups

Gerald E. Splinter, former pastor of Grant Memorial Baptist Church in Winnipeg, the largest Baptist church in Canada, had been scheduled to be at a missions conference in another city. Splinter usually flew his airplane to speaking engagements. The mission council was determining where the workers would be assigned for the next three years. He had to be there, but flying conditions were marginal. The Aeronautic Aviation Commission was advising all aircraft to stay out of the air.

An hour away from his destination, Splinter flew into a snowstorm and the plane crashed, killing him instantly.

"Why did God take him?" was the reply at the funeral. The mission director prayed, "Lord, we don't understand Your will; but we accept the things You send."

Did God send death? Did God snuff out a fruitful servant in the middle of his ministry? Or did the man's foolish decision thwart God's will for his life? No one will ever know.

The book of Job records the story of Satan appearing before God and talking about Job.

Satan said, in essence, "Job is Your child because You have made him wealthy. You have put a hedge about him and his house, and blessed his work. If You were to take away his possessions, he would curse You to Your face."

Responding to Satan, the Lord said, "Everything he owns is in your power. However, you must not lay a hand on Job himself" (Job 1:12).

Satan left the presence of God and inflicted great financial calamity on Job, and later God permitted Satan to inflict Job physically.

In the midst of the trials Job testified, "The Lord gives, and the Lord takes away" (Job 1:21). Here Job yielded himself to God, who ruled his life. However, Job's words were not quite correct. The Lord had not taken from Job; he had *permitted Satan* to take away his prosperity and health.

God's directive will was to bless Job with family, happiness, and prosperity. This is seen when Satan indicated that Job got everything from God. Later God permitted loss of family, possessions, and health. Therefore if God permits things to come to one's life, can he blame God for taking those things away? The loss of a loved one, an auto accident, or failure in school is only permitted by God.

A missionary returned home to Canada from Africa broken in health. The congregation shook their head in amazement. How could his cancelling his missionary service be God's will? The problem was that the young missionary had neglected his health. He had not slept enough, nor eaten properly, and as a result his health was broken down.

However, when he returned home, his family was consoled by knowing "that all things work together for the good of those who love God" (Rom 8:28). Is this an explanation for all human failures?

God has laws for the physical body: seven or eight hours of sleep each night, so many calories per day, and so much liquid. If a person breaks the laws of God concerning health, can anyone blame God for a broken body?

Many Christians yield their lives up to circumstances and blame God when nothing happens. To walk with God believers must "fight the good fight" for "night is coming when no one can work" (John 9:4). People cannot expect to wait for life and God's perfect will to come to them. They must lay hold, ask, and strive. God's will is revealed to those who seek it.

A small mission started in the north end of Winnipeg, Canada. The people met on Sunday mornings and attempted to establish a biblical testimony for God. The leaders were very dedicated, spiritual, and serious about reaching their neighborhood for Christ. They felt that God would touch the hearts in answer to prayer. But in essence they yielded the progress of their Sunday school mission to circumstances. They did no advertising, no evangelism, no reaching out to the neighborhood.

No one from the neighborhood attended. So after six months the doors closed on the last service and the building was put up for rent. Some Christians said it was not God's will to establish a testimony in that neighborhood. However, was this God's fault or man's fault?

Here again one can see that the will of God and the law of God go hand in hand. God has set down laws of communication. One person communicates to another through the five senses (sight, hearing, touch, taste, and smell). These five senses are the windows of the soul and no communication can go from one person to another except through these five senses. One cannot break God's laws and expect God to work.

The Sunday school mission failed because the people did not communicate its existence to the neighborhood. A church must follow the basic laws of communication or advertisement to survive and reach its clientele. To break the laws is to fail God's purpose.

God's will is reflected in the laws He has set down. God's laws are reflected in arithmetic or the order of the universe. God's laws are appreciated by the mixture of colors in an oil painting or in the order followed by a pianist playing a concert.

The missionary in northern Canada took off to fly and keep an appointment in marginal weather conditions. Yet he was warned by the Aeronautic Aviation Commission not to take off.

People asked, "Why did God take him?" The answer is simple. He broke the laws of God. God could have performed one of two miracles (a miracle is a supernatural transcending of God's laws). First, God could have transcended the laws of the storm and caused the pilot to ride out the turbulent weather. Or second, God could have raised the missionary from the dead. Either action of God would have been a miracle. Christians who heard of the death of the missionary felt that God should have guided the plane through the storm. But none expected God to raise him from the dead. It would be just as inconceivable to expect God to guide the plane through the storm as it would be to expect God to raise the dead. God could do both, but no one expects Him to raise the dead today. So how can one expect God to guide a Christian through a snowstorm when he is breaking God's laws? Therefore the death of the pilot was permitted by God, just as the broken health of the missionary to Africa was permitted by God.

The directive will of God is reflected in the laws of the world and in Scripture. The world reflects natural laws, and the Bible reflects spiritual laws. Just as a Christian cannot go against the laws of nature (e.g., falling out of a tree) and not suffer the consequences, so a Christian cannot go against the laws of God's Word without suffering the consequences.

God's will (spiritual) is written by the pen of inspired writers and is found in the pages of Scripture. God's will (natural) is found reflected in the world. Perhaps more Christians could walk in God's will by leaving their own feelings and following the facts of Scripture.

When believers know that God has a perfect will for them, they should seek to know it, and strive to do it. Paul prayed for the people in Colosse, "We are asking that you may be filled with the knowledge of His will" (Col 1:9). That means the will of God is something believers must search to know and do. As Jesus said, "If anyone wants to do His will, he will understand" (John 7:17).

As God looks to the future, nothing we do surprises Him. Even before things happen, God knows everything that people will do. Like an engineer drawing a complex blueprint that details all the functions he intends for his final product, so God has drawn the blueprint of people's lives. The believer's responsibility is to do the will of God.

DISCUSSION QUESTIONS

1. Which of the following two statements is correct, and why? (a) "God has a plan for the small details of my life." (b) "God has a plan only for the big events in my life."
2. Sometimes a person has made decisions that were not God's will for his life, and yet at the time he did not know he was missing God's plan. Why does a person not know God's will?
3. Sometimes a person has made a major decision that was in the will of God, though he did not know that at the time. How can a person know something is God's plan for his life?
4. How can a person find God's will for his life? Put the

following principles in order of importance, explaining why that particular order.

a. Common sense
b. Circumstances
c. Getting guidance from someone else (a friend or respected leader)
d. Prayer
e. Fasting
f. Bible study
g. Inner motivation from the Holy Spirit
h. Yielding to do God's will
i. Researching to get more information
j. Considering the consequences of the decision or action
k. Considering the decision in light of one's life goals
l. Asking, "How will this decision help me?"

5. When a person gets out of God's will, what can he do to get back in the center of God's will?

Endnotes

1. B. Bright, "How to Know God Personally," *Campus Crusade for Christ International*, available at http://www.ccci.org/how-to-know-god/would-you-like-to-know-god-personally/index.htm (accessed August 11, 2010).

2. "Ethics and the Will of God: The Legacy of Dietrich Bonhoeffer," *Speaking of Faith*, available at http://speakingoffaith.publicradio.org/programs/bonhoeffer/particulars.html (accessed August 11, 2010).

3. J. Piper, "What Is the Will of God and How Do We Know It?."

4. Ibid.

5. T. Strandberg, "Fate, Luck and the Will of God," *Rapture Ready*, available at http://www.raptureready.com/rr-flw.html (accessed August 11, 2010).

6. R. C. Sproul, "The Will of God," available at http://www.monergism.com/thethreshold/articles/onsite/wills_sproul.html (accessed August 11, 2010).

7. "The Will of God," *Wikipedia*, available at http://en.wikipedia.org/wiki/Will_of_God (accessed August 11, 2010).

8. Strandberg, "Fate, Luck and the Will of God."

9. J. Piper, "What Is the Will of God and How Do We Know It?," *Desiring God*, available at http://www.desiringgod.org/ResourceLibrary/Sermons/ByDate/2004/179_What_Is_the_Will_of_God_and_How_Do_We_Know_It (accessed August 11, 2010).

Conclusion:
Truth in Real Life

by Alex McFarland

A memorable encounter for me recently took place at a large church in Edmonton, Canada. I had given a presentation on the evidence for Christianity, during which I said to the audience, "Intellectual skepticism is virtually always preceded by emotional pain." I explained that (in my experience, at least) people who are very skeptical of Christianity are actually *hurting*. Show me someone who nurtures his doubts, props up his unbelief with one argument after another, and I'll show you an individual who has probably allowed emotional pain to come between him and God.

At the end of my talk a female graduate student walked over to me. "I don't fit your profile," she said. "My lack of faith is not due to any pain or trauma. I think that God is often a crutch for people who need something to believe in."

As the young woman and I began to talk, about 20 other college students lingered around us, listening. The woman insisted that her skepticism was based on pure, unbiased rationality, not driven by any underlying emotional factors. For a few minutes we talked about some of the basic evidences for God's existence. She had a reason for rejecting each of my attempts to show the plausibility of Christianity, but she repeatedly thanked me for taking time to engage her in the conversation.

When I felt that it was appropriate in the conversation, I asked two questions. Having had many such conversations with skeptics before, I knew that her answers would give me insight into how I might best minister to her.

"Have you always questioned God's existence, or was there ever a time that you did believe?" My other "question" was really more of a request: "Tell me about your background, your home life growing up."

These are intensely personal questions, and I recommend that these questions be asked of someone only if a significant level of trust is present in the conversation. As the woman was about to answer me, her eyes darted momentarily toward the other college students overhearing our conversation. For a second I thought she might want to end the discussion. "Don't worry about them," she said. "Most of them are my friends, and some of them work hard to try to convert me." Gentle laughter came from the audience for a brief moment.

As for my two questions, the woman explained that as a child she had believed that there was a God who loved her. She talked about spending some of her childhood years with a relative near Alberta, Canada, and talking to God during outdoor walks. Her reminiscences fast-forwarded to her late teens, by which time she had abandoned belief in God. As an excellent student in both high school and college, she began to find self-worth (and life's answers) in academics. Her studies would prepare her for a career in medical research.

"What was your family life like during all those years?" I asked. "Not so great," she said. "Part of the reason my brother and I were living temporarily with an aunt in Banff was so that we would be shielded from some rough stuff happening during our parents' breakup." She went on to explain that her father had a problem with alcohol and often became abusive without warning. Episodes of verbal abuse eventually escalated into physical abuse, at which time the woman's mother gathered the children and left.

"When is the last time you've spoken to your dad?" I asked. "It's been years," she replied. "And I don't plan on seeing him anytime soon. I am pretty much past all that now." I detected a hint of anger in her voice as she spoke.

Meeting People at Their Point of Need

In listening to the young woman speaking with me there, I was reminded of some profound observations made by Edith Schaeffer, wife of Christian thinker Francis Schaeffer. Shortly before her husband's death in 1985, Mrs. Schaeffer said, "The family is the church in miniature. It is in the home that we learn our first lessons about love, forgiveness, authority, obedience, grace." She added, "The home was designed by God to prepare our hearts for the gospel."

Many of the people around us who have negative images of their *heavenly Father* harbor painful memories of their *earthly* fathers. I have met some people who experienced situations growing up that resulted in their becoming virtually inoculated against faith in God. Negative church experiences can have similar results, leaving a formerly dedicated and loving person alienated and bitter after the trauma. Years of reaching out to skeptics and atheists have led me to conclude that the more tender and committed a person is before some emotional trauma, the more hostile and antithetical he will become after having jettisoned his faith.

After hearing the college student in Canada tell about her abusive upbringing, I said, "I know that you told me you did not think you fit the typical 'skeptics profile.' But is it not possible that pain from your past has influenced your view of God?" We continued to talk and the other students continued to listen. So that she and the other college students could hear, I explained what it means to have a relationship with Christ. I challenged the young woman to honestly consider my belief that her skepticism was a means of managing the pain of negative past experiences. To use a medical analogy I said, "For some people, emotional hurts and anger metastasize into unbelief. God can heal this, if the patient is willing."

She smiled and thanked me several times for speaking with her. She did not pray the sinner's prayer in the auditorium at the end of that evening, but that is OK. We both listened to each other, and she accepted the book I offered her. Driving out of the parking lot, I saw that she was sitting in her car with the interior light on, reading my book. I have prayed for her often since then.

Four Realities of Twenty-First-Century Ministry

1. The number of people with recurring spiritual doubts will continue to grow in the Western world.
2. Those with spiritual doubts increasingly defy categorization. For example I meet "atheists" who say that they frequently pray. Or those who claim to be Christians but who study a variety of "holy books" and not just the Bible. Familiar labels do not work much any more.
3. Building reciprocal, authentic relationships—though

time-consuming—is the *key* to helping lead people into an authentic, saving relationship with Jesus Christ.

4. Familiarity with apologetics is a necessity in ministering to twenty-first-century pagans. In the initial phase of evangelization, "relationship" seems to trump "content." But at some point during the conversation (after much trust has been built), theological "content" will become as important as "relationship." The most fruitful evangelizers and disciplers will be Christians who have both social *and* apologetic savvy.

I still maintain that: intellectual skepticism is preceded by emotional pain. I have observed many examples of individuals going to great lengths to justify their unbelief in spite of known evidence for God and Christianity. C. S. Lewis candidly described the mental gymnastics that accompanies willful unbelief: "I was at that time living like many atheists, in a whirl of contradictions. I maintained that God did not exist. I was also very angry with God for not existing. I was equally angry with him for creating a world."[1]

Pain can cause unbelief to grip a person's heart and mind. But there are counter-examples, as the following story shows.

Pain Does Not Have to Be Spiritually Debilitating

Stephanie's dad was a pastor in a small rural community. She grew up among friendly neighbors, sang in the youth choir, and attended a local school small enough for just about every one to be on a first-name basis. She could not imagine a future anything less than the idyllic one she had always known.

A more harsh reality began to insert itself when her dad walked out on his marriage of 30 years and pastorate of 15 years.

Stephanie's family was devastated, and the little community watched in shock as a trusted "man of God" left his wife for one of the church members. "I saw my father say and do things that I would have never thought possible," Stephanie said. "The affair, their appearances together in public—it was so painful for our family, embarrassing for the church, and it just rocked our community."

Deeply painful situations that come on people abruptly become defining moments. How a person processes such circumstances shapes him for years to come. For a "preacher's kid" in her late teens, Stephanie's situation could have been what I call "spiritually terminal." Emerging from the rubble of life's implosions leave some as bitter skeptics.

Stephanie said, "I remember lying on the floor just wishing I could die. I felt anger toward my dad and anger toward God. But eventually I realized that this was not God's fault. My dad made the decision to walk away. I realized I now had to make a decision in light of my dad's decision."

As the agonizing months of a family breakup dragged on, Stephanie began to understand that her reaction to it all would profoundly shape her future. She says,

> I asked myself, "Will I, like my dad, turn my back on my faith, my life, and all I knew to be true?" This became the defining moment of my life, so far. I was hurting, but at the same time I knew that many facts affirm that Christianity is true. Jesus Christ *did* live, die, and rise again. Looking back, I remembered times that God has answered prayer and provided for my needs. The healing of my emotions began when I made the mental choice to trust God even in this deep valley. As I made the decision

to trust God, I felt His presence as never before. Even though some days are still emotionally challenging, the sense of peace God gave me has never left, and my walk with Christ has grown stronger since then.

Stephanie's story is a good example of how to process one's pain in a way that is both redemptive and healthy. But it is also an example of how apologetics content (in this case, knowledge that Christ's life is rooted in historical fact) can bolster one's faith when a person's world is rocked by unforeseen tragedy.

Where Do We Go from Here?

This book began by saying that good questions demand good answers. The book has sought to give answers that are both *reasonable* and *relevant*. If you began this book with doubts about Christianity, our challenge to you is to act on what you have just read. Turn to God in repentance and faith. Embark on the greatest adventure possible: become a follower of Jesus Christ. To know Him is the meaning of life and of eternity!

If you are a Christian, here is a "call to action" for you: get busy *presenting, explaining,* and (when necessary) *defending* your faith. True discipleship means loving God *and* one's neighbors with not just the heart, but also the mind.

Some may assume that the study of theology and apologetics is for the "ivory tower" and is not practical for everyday life. Not so! Apologetics is very practical because it helps nurture two very important parts of the Christian life: *evangelism* and *discipleship*. Apologetics is immeasurably practical because it contributes to persuasion of the lost and the maturing of the saved.

Ever since becoming a Christian 25 years ago, I have studied apologetics. Shortly after my conversion I began to purchase works by authors whose names (at the time) were unfamiliar to me, but the content of their books looked interesting—names like Josh McDowell, Chuck Colson, Francis Schaeffer, and C. S. Lewis.

By the fall of 1985, after having been a Christian for only three months, I was convinced that the future of the American church *must* involve apologetics, I knew that it would define my own future as well. Within one year of becoming a Christian, I owned 100 books on apologetics and the Christian worldview, and I had read the Bible intensively. Why? So that I could "blow the doors off" of any opponent in a discussion? Of course not!

I had become passionate about internalizing Scripture and becoming proficient about sharing God's truth with others. I had initially bought a book of answers to common questions by evangelist Billy Graham because I wanted to tell my college buddies about Jesus Christ. Before getting saved, I ran with a hard-living, hard-drinking crowd of guys. A couple of our peers had even died in drunk-driving-related auto accidents. Moments after the euphoria of conversion began to sink in, I was pondering the spiritual condition of my best friends with great concern. When I began to tell them about Christ, they listened to a degree but also peppered me with questions.

Studying apologetics equipped me to give reasonable answers to my friends' questions, and I began to see fruit for my evangelistic efforts. Looking back to those times in the mid-1980s, I believe that my experiences on college campuses provided great training for the cultural contexts that awaited me in the years to come.

The college I was then attending is known for an arts department and film school that draws many students from across the country. Even Stephen Spielberg came and spoke on campus one year, along with other opinion makers as well. As a young Christian, I found myself talking with people who were clueless as to what the gospel is. At other times I shared Christ with people who were openly hostile to "the organized church" (such as a group of political activists who owned a gay bookstore across from the campus). But in the years that have gone by since then, I have not really heard any new questions beyond the basic ones I learned to face in those formative years. People want to know why Christians think they have a handle on absolute truth. In one way or another people will call on believers to defend their belief that Christianity is authentic. But most of all, I have found that people want to see if the Christian is authentic. Christians often care most about showing that their *message* is authentic, but the unsaved want to be sure that the *messenger* is authentic.

Believers who witness for Christ will find, as I did, that they will be asked questions like these: How do we know there is a God? Is the Bible really true? What makes Jesus so special? Did He *really* rise from the grave? The most gnawing issue for most skeptics is the question, Why does God (if He exists and really does love us) allow all of these bad things to go on in the world?

I went into apologetics in order to make an impact on the lives of those around me. But as I read, studied, and prayed, I noticed that the one who was being changed was *me*. I often found myself praising God for revealing Himself and wonderful truths to fallen (and often thankless) creatures. Learning more and more about God's attributes, I found myself praising God for who He is. My point is that apologetics is more than a useful tool for persuasion of the lost. Apologetics can foster growth and spiritual maturity in the believer's life, along with deeper intimacy with Christ.

Much of apologetics study will stretch one's mind, but it should also enlarge his heart. The Bible states that the gospel is not based on "cleverly devised fables" (2 Pet 1:16), but it also says that changed lives and godly actions speak loudly to an often skeptical world (1 Pet 2:15). Apologetics is more than dialoguing with people. It is about loving God and loving people. What could be more practical than that?

Traversing What Looks like "A Smooth Green Meadow"

Charlotte, North Carolina, has a fairly impressive skyline. Walking through the Concourse E breezeway at Charlotte's local airport, people can look out the window and see a beautiful view of the city skyline. Charlotte's skyscrapers can be seen in the distance on the other side of what looks like a large expanse of grass. From this vantage point Charlotte's downtown looks like the distant Emerald City in a scene from the *Wizard of Oz*. It appears as if one could stroll across the grassy expanse and walk directly there.

What a person cannot see, though, is that lying between Concourse E and downtown are deep gullies of rocks and vines, a couple of major highways, and about 15 miles of rough terrain. The point? What looks on the surface like an easy stroll would actually be a tough journey to make. It is that way with helping some people find Christ.

Christians may assume, "The gospel is true, and the evidence is in our favor, and so why should people not believe?" Correct. But according to 1 John 1: 5–10, people have *bias* and *blindness*. For some, years of willful unbelief result in a state of spiritual *bondage*. This bondage can take different forms in the lives of different individuals, but ultimately the same basic problems are present: pride and deceit (both self and with others). First John 1:8–10 warns, "If we say, 'We have no sin,' we are deceiving ourselves, and the truth is not in us. . . . If we say, 'We have not sinned,' we make Him a liar, and His word is not in us."

Skeptics and Seekers

Nonbelievers may be grouped into two categories: skeptics and seekers. Skeptics are people who think they need to hear all the fancy answers to their difficult questions.

Tim Downs says, "True courage resists the fear of being thought a coward and seeks to communicate out of love and justice. Sometimes, courage is not telling the unbeliever everything he needs to hear; sometimes, it's telling him only what he can bear."[2] Colossians 4:5–6 says, "Walk in wisdom toward outsiders, making the most of the time. Your speech should always be gracious, seasoned with salt, so that you may know how you should answer each person." Allow the Holy Spirit to guide you in talking to unbelievers and in enabling you to ascertain what each person needs to hear. Some people do need answers, while others just need truth in love.

Isaiah 59:15–16a says, "Truth is missing, and whoever turns from evil is plundered. The LORD saw that there was no justice, and He was offended. He saw that there was no man—He was amazed that there was no one interceding." Truth may be lacking, but there are still people to intercede. Believers need to stand up for God and intercede, to bring truth to a truthless world and shine the light of the gospel.

The Importance of Tackling the Tough Questions

As assistant pastor of a large Methodist church located near a dozen colleges, Keith Lowder understands the importance of students being grounded in their knowledge of Scripture. He has seen the struggles that arise in the lives of young adults when they lack adequate Bible knowledge.

Keith said, "I've worked with a lot of twenty-somethings who may have been part of a strong youth group during high school, but were unprepared for the challenges that college life throws at their Christian worldview. Tough questions about certain Bible passages are a struggle for many. Young adults frequently elevate experience above Scripture anyway. But when trust in the Bible goes, this becomes the norm."[3]

Nothing Exempted in the Culture of Doubt

A number of recent media releases are contributing to people's doubts about Christianity and the Bible. Many websites (some of which are intentionally aimed at youth) are devoted to debunking the Bible. Books like *The God Delusion,* by Richard Dawkins, and *Misquoting Jesus,* by Bart Ehrmann, have "the new atheism," along with questions about the Bible's integrity.

Many of the questions raised by these high-profile skeptics are on the minds of youth and college students I meet. People of all ages want to know, Can the Bible stand up to serious scrutiny?

Doubts and questions about God and the Bible are nothing new. Every generation has its share of critics who attempt to prove that the Bible contradicts itself. The good news is that virtually every conceivable quibble over the problem passages was plausibly answered long ago. There have always been skeptics. Some are bright and sincere, but they are misguided or unwilling to embrace the truth once they have encountered it. Others simply have an ax to grind.

Many of the questions being raised by high-profile skeptics are also on the minds of people I meet. Having traveled extensively throughout the county over the last 20 years, I have come to understand that doubters fall into one of several categories. I have found that there are usually some unique aspects to each skeptic's position. Identifying what type of skepticism is *really* present—and interacting with a person in light of this—can dramatically change the result of how a person responds to the Christian faith.

Reaching Out to the Skeptics Around Us

Some skeptics are natural "questioners," who truly are seeking answers. They will often raise spiritual conundrums out of genuine curiosity, hoping that a believer can shed a little light on their confusion (e. g., "I have often wondered how you can believe in the virgin birth").

Other skeptics are what I call "passively noncommittal" when it comes to spiritual issues. Regarding the "God question," these people seem to be ambivalent. They chafe at spiritual truth without being either curious or confrontational about it. If we know this person and his philosophical bent, we will need to invest extra effort to initiate a spiritual dialogue ("Are you a geology major. What do you think about the fossil record as it relates to life on earth?").

Still other skeptics are more outspoken. An established relationship is not a prerequisite for reaching out to an aggressive skeptic, but it helps. All the aggressive skeptic needs is to overhear someone talking about the Bible, and it pushes his or her buttons ("You Christians think you know it all. What makes you think your view is more correct than any other religion?").

Understanding the Person with Whom You Speak

Is the person:	Then his need is generally:
A searcher?	informational, evidential
A skeptic?	relational
Is the issue:	**Then his struggle is probably about:**
A question?	answers
An objection?	authority

One of the more aggressive skeptics I have seen recently was in a Starbucks coffee shop in my hometown of Charlotte, North Carolina. Four or five men were gathered around a table quietly having a morning devotional together. I noticed a man sitting nearby, watching, and apparently trying to figure out what the group was doing. Suddenly, the man began to call out (in a less-than-conversational tone), "Bull----! Bull----!" Every few minutes the man would call out, "Religion is bull----," or something similar.

I watched the mood in the bustling Starbucks become very awkward, as the group stared down at their Bibles, and the man spoke periodic epithets from behind a newspaper. In a few moments the group of men quietly packed up and left the Starbucks. They did the right thing. Believers should resist getting defensive with someone like this and try not to take the verbal assault personally.

Let Me Say It Again: *Intellectual Skepticism Is Preceded by Pain*

Almost all the atheists I have spoken with tell war stories from the days when they used to be in church. One college student who proudly introduced herself as an "ex-Christian" had begun to question God after prayers for a cancer-stricken loved one seemed to go unanswered. In loving and ministering to such people, empathy, discernment, and a listening ear will take the conversation much further than a data dump.

Just recently a teen (only 15 years old) told me, "If the God of the Bible exists, I've never seen Him." A dozen possible apologetic responses came to mind, but I put them all on the back burner. The teen told me that his hero was the atheist, Christopher Hitchens. As he began to list his problems with God and Christianity, I asked, "Why the big push-back against God? What happened?" He gave me a guarded look and replied, "You really want to know? This could take a while." As our talk stretched into more than an hour, the teen's militant posture of unbelief began to wane. I listened to his story of a family tragedy that was compounded by the uncaring (and unscriptural) response of the church they attended at the time.

At the end of more than two hours of conversation (most of which involved my listening), the teen tearfully prayed a prayer of recommitment to Christ. It dawned on me that God's work in this young man's life had little to do with any apologetics evidence that I shared. As far as I could tell, what began to melt his tough façade was that I cared enough to take time to listen. Of course data and content matter. But as important as it is to be ready with an answer for the hope we have (1 Pet 3:15), effective outreach to skeptics is probably about 80 percent "relationship" and 20 percent "persuasive evidence."

With friendliness and a winsome spirit, Christians should try to connect with the persons God places in their paths. I suggest the following to those who are serious about talking with those who have doubts. Find a quiet place where you can both open up. Ask questions such as, "Have you always felt this way, or did something happen that caused you to change your beliefs?" Listen carefully to the other person's position, trying to discern the real obstacle to faith. Restate what the person said so that you are sure you really understand.

Psychologists have long noted that true relationships are *reciprocal*. There should be positive "give and take," which on one or more levels is mutually beneficial. Establishing and nurturing an actual relationship is vitally important if meaningful dialogue with a skeptic is to take place. In talking with skeptics three characteristics must be present: *trust, honesty,* and *respect.*

Christians are representatives of Jesus Christ. The assumptions people have about God and Christianity are influenced by how believers act and by what they say. Christians should employ good arguments, but should never become argumentative. Believers should resist the temptation to point a one-way "firehose" of information on listeners. The conversation should be steered toward the subject of Jesus, just as the Lord did when talking with the Samaritan woman in John 4:1–26. Ancillary issues often fade away when the discussion focuses on Christ. Even as the believer is talking, he silently prays for the Holy Spirit to be at work in the situation.

The book *God in the Dock,* by C. S. Lewis, implies that people attempt to keep God on the witness stand. They consider the Bible guilty until proven innocent. Some of the more vitriolic skeptics say they have come from churches where questions and critical thinking were off limits. This is sad because one duty of Christians is to worship God through continual nurture of the intellect (Matt 22:37; Rom 12:2). Nevertheless a Christian's goal should never be to win arguments. Believers are simply called on to testify in hopes of convincing skeptics to consider the facts with an open mind and allow the Scriptures to vindicate themselves under cross-examination.

Bible-detractors in our day are effectively spreading their message of doubt through popular books, skeptic's Web sites, and YouTube content. Many of the individuals impacted by these apologists of unbelief are inquisitive young adults. Skeptics of all ages should know that there are solid answers for the tough questions. But they will not find them in trendy books, YouTube rants, or babbling blogs. It is up to reasoned, respectful Christians to point them in the right direction.

We May *Attempt,* but God Actually *Does*

In 1807 missionary Robert Morrison met with then-president James Madison. Morrison was en route to China, where he would become the first Protestant missionary to that nation. "Do you really expect to make an impression on the great Chinese Empire?" asked Madison. Morrison replied, "No, sir, but I expect God will."

The prospect of presenting, explaining, and defending the faith before a doubting twenty-first-century world may seem daunting. If believers depend on only their abilities, the task *would* be impossible. But believers can be encouraged by the realization that God's power and providence are the "engines" on which evangelism runs. Christians have a great responsibility to present Christ effectively in a culture of increasing spiritual darkness. At the same time it is very liberating to remember that people, cultures, and all of history are in the hands of the sovereign God.

The Russian author Leo Tolstoy spent much time as a young adult wrestling with the following questions: Why am I living? What is the cause of my existence? Why do I exist? Why is there a division of good and evil with me? How must I live? What is death—and how can I save myself? People today are pondering the very same "ultimate issues." It is part of being human.

One's next-door neighbor may verbalize it differently or not at all. But his soul longs to know where we came from, why we are here, and where we are going. He may not have arranged his questions and currently held positions into neat categories (reading apologetics books leads people to do things like that), but everyone wonders about God, truth, creation, man, morals, life's purpose, pain, history, and eternity. Respectfully and to the best of their ability, Christians must help others arrive at biblically informed positions on worldview issues.

Endnotes

1. C. S. Lewis, *Surprised by Joy* (New York: Harcourt Brace, 1995), 111.

2. T. Downs, *Finding Common Ground* (Chicago: Moody, 1999), 7.

3. K. Lowder interviewed by Alex McFarland on June 28, 2008.

Subject and Name Index

Scripture Index